# PROBLEM SOLVING in SCHOOL SCIENCE

## Robert Johnsey

*Deputy Head*
*Reaside Middle School*
*Frankley*

Macdonald Educational

A MACDONALD BOOK

Text © Robert Johnsey 1986
Artwork © Macdonald & Co (Publishers) Ltd 1986
Photographs © Fiona Pragoff, Robert Johnsey and
Steve Fretwell 1986

First published in Great Britain in 1986
Reprinted 1987

Printed and bound in Great Britain by
A. Wheaton & Co Ltd
Exeter

A BPCC plc company

Published in Great Britain by
Macdonald & Co (Publishers) Ltd
Hampstead Road
London NW1 7QX

A BPCC plc company

British Library Cataloguing in Publication Data
Johnsey, Robert
    Problem solving in school science.
    1. Science—Study and teaching (Secondary)—
    Great Britain
    I. Title
    507'.1241        Q183.4.G7

    ISBN 0-356-11322-1

### Acknowledgements
The author would like to acknowledge the importance of
his association with the Secondary Science Curriculum
Review and the contribution that the Redditch SSCR
group has made to the development of the ideas in this
book.

### Photograph credits
Cover: Robert Johnsey and Steve Fretwell
Page 15: Robert Johnsey
All other photographs by Fiona Pragoff

### Photocopying
The worksheets on pages 14, 16, 29, 37, 40, 48, 53
and 57 may be photocopied in their entirety without
payment or the need to seek specific permission
from the author or the publisher in the following
cases: (a) multiple copies for use in teaching;
(b) single copies for the purpose of private study
or research only. In all other cases, including the
rest of the text and the illustrations, permission
must be sought.

Editors:       Diana Forster and John Day
Designer:      David Minchin
Illustrator:   Jeff Edwards/Marlborough Design
Production:    John Moulder and Ken Holt

# Contents

## Introduction

## 1. Elastic Energy

## 2. Seeds on the Move

## 3. Time

## 4. Wheels

## 5. Paper Structures

## Index

# Introduction

This book is about setting children open-ended problems with a predominantly scientific content.

Perhaps, too often, we as teachers make all the decisions for our children with the intention that they will learn to make choices for themselves in the future when they have gained sufficient experience. We might question, however, if this is really the case.

When and where will children learn to have confidence in their own decisions? How will they come to develop the positive self-image they need in order to solve their own problems? It is tempting to leave even the simplest problems to the 'experts'. Should we not be encouraging youngsters of all ages to be inventive and to use their initiative in solving problems of all kinds, to make up their minds about selected matters and to gain that special confidence that comes from overcoming difficulties without adult help?

This book suggests how a teacher might set practical challenges to a class of children in order to achieve these aims.

We begin with a story.

It was a cold winter's day, so the heating fan was bound to be on. But to the annoyance of Mr Goodman and his class, it was spoiling their experiment.

A few days before, the question of hearing ability had been discussed by the children and now every one was absorbed in finding out who had the best hearing in the class. Today they needed a quiet classroom in which to try out some ideas.

The design of the experiment had given everyone much to think about. Darren had suggested that they measure everyone's ears to see whose were the biggest. Mr Goodman pointed out that this would make him the certain 'winner' so they all thought again. Julie's idea was to play a cassette tape with simple French conversation and see who could understand what was being said. This plunged the class into a discussion about the difference between hearing well and understanding what we hear.

Omar's suggestion was that someone should whisper a word at the far side of the room and the subject of the test has to repeat it. This threw up a number of problems such as: 'cat' would be easy to hear and repeat but what about 'catastrophe'? This idea, however, had set everyone on the right track and eventually the class came to the conclusion that one way of testing hearing ability was to use a source of sound that was both consistent and fairly quiet. If they could increase the sound step by step until it was heard, then they would have some measure of hearing ability.

Mr Goodman knew that one of the pleasant things about asking children to design experiments of their own is that one never knows quite what to expect. Often the simplest ideas are the most effective and

may not be foreseen by a teacher who may have been brought up on a diet of prescriptive science lessons.

**1** Design for a hearing test

The children set about designing their experiments. Lucie was a quiet, thoughtful girl. Her work was not generally outstanding but now she provided one of those imaginative ideas that Mr Goodman enjoyed. She decided to use the fall of a piece of card on to a table as her source of sound. The set of identical cards were arranged at equal intervals extending away from the listener. The card furthest away was dropped first and a few seconds allowed to lapse. Then the next was released and so on until the subject indicated that he had heard the card. His score was recorded as the number of the card that he heard. Obviously, if the indication came at a time when no card was dropped then this was discounted.

**2** The hearing test in operation

Mr Goodman decided to try the test on members of the class with everyone making their own record of the results. They had all discussed, at length, the need to be fair to each 'contestant' and today they decided that if the heating fan stayed on all the time it would at least be the same for everyone!

The tests were carried out on each individual in

the class. There was a slight technical hitch at the beginning when it was discovered that if the card was cushioned by air as it fell, then it made practically no sound at all. This problem was overcome by folding over one corner of each card so that it met the table first with a slight tap.

Once the tests were complete, Mr Goodman's class sat back with a feeling of satisfaction. It had been interesting. The results were there on paper for all to see. The 'winner' was Jamie Hardcastle. Mr Goodman, however, was worried by this rather comfortable state of euphoria.

Were there no complaints? Can we be absolutely satisfied with these results? Does Jamie really have the best hearing? Ought we not to check these results, perhaps by using another type of test?

It was at this point that Sally took courage and complained that when her friend Susan was tested, one or two cards had been dropped from a lower position and thus made a softer sound. Had they been dropped differently, perhaps Susan would have heard these cards and gained a better score. Matthew then said that the first card of Jamie's that he had heard immediately, had fallen awkwardly, making a louder noise than usual. Others in the class, now shaken out of their complacency, joined the good-natured debate.

The conclusion was that a New Improved Test was needed with emphasis on the way in which the sound was produced.

Mr Goodman decided to help his children define the new problem they had set themselves. In order to devise a fair hearing test, we need something that makes a quiet sound that remains the same no matter how many times we use it. If this device is portable, we could move it closer and closer to the subject of the test until he or she first hears it. The 'score', then, will be the distance in centimetres between the subject and the sound device.

It was a few days later that Mr Goodman and his class returned to the problem. He introduced them to the idea of 'brainstorming': 'Throw in any ideas that are remotely connected with the problem and do not worry about how ridiculous they may seem at first.'

*Get someone to hum at the same level all the time.*
What if he or she runs out of puff at the crucial moment?

*Someone could drag a foot on the floor as he or she approached the subject.*
You cannot rely on a person to always make the same sound.

*Use a radio turned down low.*
But perhaps music is easier to hear than talking.

*An electric bell. A food mixer. An alarm clock.*
Too loud.

*An alarm clock in a cardboard box.*
*An alarm clock wrapped in a blanket in a cardboard box!*

Having decided that they could not rely on a person to make sounds of a consistent level, the children agreed that it would have to be a 'machine' of some description. It was at this point that Mr Goodman set his children to make their own sound device using the bits and pieces available in the classroom. He knew to a certain extent where he was leading his class, so a variety of materials were on hand in labelled boxes. The children's task had now temporarily changed from the design of an experiment to the design and construction of a working model. From being purely scientists, the children were now taking on the role of technologists, too.

**3** Making a soft-sound machine

Once the children had put their ideas on paper in the form of labelled diagrams, they went on to make a wide range of sound devices. From Royston who used two card tubes that rubbed against each other to Dawn who used a spring-loaded trigger striking on a plastic dish, each design was different and had the children totally absorbed.

Mr Goodman and his class returned, eventually, to the hearing tests with the best of the inventions and proceeded to establish some quite reliable results. He made a point of playing down the actual results — they were of little importance. What was valuable was the way in which the children, in their various ways, had arrived at them.

## The two processes

This story of Mr Goodman and his class illustrates two processes — two ways of working — which are different but closely related. One is that of the pure scientist in which a question is posed and answered by experiment. The other is the process of design technology involving the solution to a problem by the design and construction of a device. While children may not need to distinguish between the two processes, it is helpful if we, as teachers, have it clear in our minds. This book is essentially about the problem solving process that a technologist might use but it is worth considering the science process briefly as the two are often closely intertwined.

A scientific approach to the world around us could be described in the way shown in figure 4.

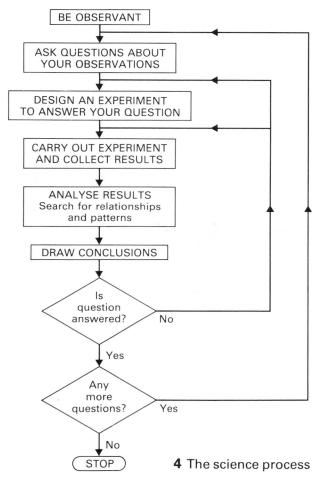

**4** The science process

In the days preceding the hearing tests, Mr Goodman's class had been following a topic on Our Senses. They noticed how different people respond to different stimuli, how hearing can be enhanced or diminished and how some people have better hearing than others. These were useful *observations* and led to a number of interesting questions, one of which was: 'Who do you think has the best hearing in the class?' This kind of question can only be answered by experiment and its value cannot be over-emphasised. Children need to be trained to ask such *questions* as it is a key part of the scientific approach. Being observant is a beginning but we must question what we observe in order to learn more.

Once Mr Goodman's class had framed their question, the way forward to *design the experiment* and gather the *results* was fairly clear. One of their *conclusions*, with suitable prompting from their teacher, was that the test was not entirely fair. As a result of this decision they returned to the design of the experiment to work through the process again, though this time with an improved method for making sounds.

Our main concern here is with the second process, that of the design technologist. It is about solving problems in the classroom with the intention that the way of working and the confidence gained will be carried into other areas of the curriculum. A framework to have in mind when asking children to solve practical problems is shown in figure 5.

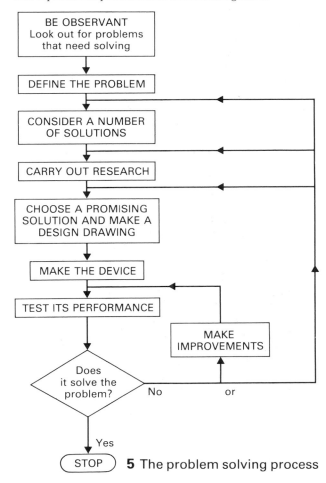

**5** The problem solving process

## Observation and definition of the problem

In Mr Goodman's hearing test, the children noticed that a more suitable sound device was necessary. Those who were less observant might have missed this fact. Mr Goodman was careful to help his children by defining the problem clearly. This is somewhat similar to setting the rules for a game. Not all problems need to be defined so precisely but it does help children to have their attention focused on a particular goal. As children become more experienced in this kind of activity, they can work with a freer brief or even define problems of their own. In this book, the problems are presented to the children in a clearly defined form. Their task, therefore, is to solve them by working through the process as follows.

## Consider a number of solutions

The brainstorming session in our story threw up a number of ideas. The crazier suggestions may have paved the way for the more practical ones. It was important that Mr Goodman accepted anything put forward at this stage — even humorous contributions. This gives hesitant members of the group the confidence to speak up because 'anything goes'.

**6** A discussion beforehand can give children the opportunity to develop their initial ideas

This initial discussion of possible solutions can give the less imaginative children time to gather their thoughts. The experienced teacher will know just how long to prolong this discussion stage. Too little input and much of the class may be left floundering not knowing how to begin. Too much and frustration may begin to creep in.

A useful technique at this stage is to ask the children to sketch, briefly, three or four different solutions to the problem. These 'doodles' give the children time to be inventive and to consider all the implications of the problem. It also gives the teacher time to head off impossible ideas as well as to enhance the children's vocabulary and communication skills.

'Let's see now. What is this squiggle here?'
'How will you support this spindle so that it can rotate?'

In the end, the important point is that we should not rush forward with the first idea that enters our head but choose the best calmly from a limited number of solutions. The preliminary discussions and doodles enable us to do just that.

## Research

Somewhere around this stage in the problem solving process it may be appropriate to introduce some research. This may take the form of reading reference books to find out how the problem has been tackled before. If, for instance, a problem is set involving the blades of a windmill, then initial reference to pictures and text in a book or wall chart might provide a useful stimulus. The children will benefit all the more from this 'book work' because it is for a tangible purpose. Experiencing the real thing would be so much more valuable than looking at pictures and reading texts. Do you have a local windmill? If you do not, take your children to the staff car park to show them the blades of the cooling fan in your car!

An important alternative method of research would be a practical scientific investigation. The children in Mr Goodman's class might have studied, for instance, the sound properties of elastic bands. This investigation would take the form of a more traditional science lesson and may be guided by instructions on a workcard or worksheet. We may even require, at this stage, a mini-experiment to find out if a particular principle works.

**7** Close observation forms part of the research before a model is constructed

One of the children in Mr Goodman's class thought of bouncing a rubber ball on to a cardboard box to produce a sound. She gave the idea a quick trial before making up her mind but discarded the idea because the sound made was not consistent enough. (If she had persevered, she might have overcome this problem but in fact she went on to use a marble falling inside a card tube.) Within this informal trial, however, we can find all the stages in the scientific process — observing, questioning, testing, gathering results (even though they may not be recorded) and drawing conclusions.

## The design drawing

Once a decision has been made as to the most promising solution to a problem, then it may be appropriate to make a labelled design drawing.

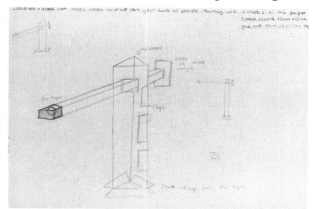

**8** The design drawing is a communication of ideas to others

Children at different stages of development will produce different degrees of sophistication in their drawings. From match-stick men to isometric, technical drawings, from comic strip to formal plan and elevation — the teacher must decide what can be expected. The purpose of the drawings, however, remains the same: the communication of ideas to others especially the teacher. This drawing, which is more detailed than the preliminary doodles, gives the child a further chance to work out ideas before becoming committed to construction.

A set of drawings will not always be necessary. The teacher must decide when emphasis is to be given to some other aspect of the design process. There are times when putting pen to paper may inhibit a child's inventiveness. Some children will find it quite difficult to visualise their model and then draw it. It may only come to life when they handle the solid materials of construction. Certainly most children will modify their paper plans as they begin to construct in three dimensions and this should be permitted.

Finally, drawings are not the only way in which to plan ahead. I once asked a group of children to invent something that would test the hardness of various kinds of wood. This involved something like measuring the indentation made by an object as it fell on to the wood or was pressed into the wood. The children missed out the drawing stage and

spent a useful afternoon making card models of their 'machines' in preparation for making the real thing. Some of the models even had working parts and, of course, showed more clearly than a drawing exactly what the children had in mind.

## Construction

What seemed simple on paper can often cause all kinds of problems in reality. But then we are in the business of solving problems and with the correct preparation you and your children can overcome most of the difficulties that come your way. It is important that children do not become disillusioned at this stage through lack of technical expertise. Some schools will have access to a craft area with facilities for using wood and metal. This opens up a great number of possibilities for construction but the projects in this book are designed for more humble surroundings. All the projects have been developed in situations in which one teacher works with a full class in a classroom or laboratory. Much use is made of card, plastic containers and wire. Scissors, glue, a pair of pliers and ingenuity are the tools of the trade. If the problems that are set are carefully arranged, then the level of inventiveness and thought that goes into them will be as high as if sophisticated materials and tools were used. Indeed, many technical problems presented to children are merely designed to give impressive results. It is often debatable how much real thinking the children are required to do. Could it be that too often they are merely required to follow the teacher's line of thought?

The problems that arise when children begin to make their models are too varied to be dealt with here. There are, however, many helpful hints and comments on predictable trouble spots in the projects that follow. With experience, teachers will be able to foresee problems of construction and take action before the children feel a sense of failure.

Recently a group of children were making paddle boats of their own design. I could foresee a major problem in fixing the paddle blades to a thin wooden axle. To avoid the wasted time and disappointment that would have been incurred if the blades had been fixed in a flimsy manner, I spent half an hour

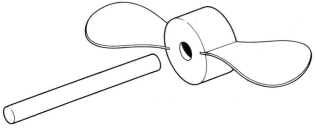

**9** An easily assembled paddle

sawing pieces from a broom handle and drilling a central hole. It was then an easy task for the children to fix their blades into these 'cotton reels' and to glue their complete paddles to the axles (figure 9).

I had solved only one of their problems and left plenty of other decisions for them to make.

## Testing and improving

When the children in Mr Goodman's class had made their sound device, they then had to put it through trials to make sure it did the job it was supposed to. Here the science process is employed once again either formally or informally: devise a fair test and analyse the results. If the sound model does not work successfully, then improvements have to be made before the whole class can use it. Children will need to be encouraged to work through the cycle:

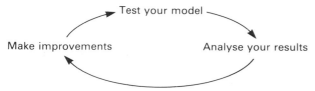

They should understand that the problem solving process never really finishes. There is always room for improvement. This idea, incidentally, is worth having in mind for those in your class who work quickly and delight in telling you that they have finished before everyone else. Encourage them to improve their model or even build a better one. Most of the projects that follow have suggestions for extension work for those who have satisfactorily completed the first challenge.

We can emphasise the improvement part of the design process by sometimes presenting children with an imperfect device and asking them to improve it. Make a simple paper aeroplane that hardly flies and challenge the children to add to the basic design until their model will 'fly' the distance across the room. When the children have analysed the deficiencies in the test flight, they may choose to add tails, flaps or paper clip weights and maybe even subtract bits from the original model.

This process that has been described is a useful framework to have in mind when asking children to solve practical problems of an open-ended nature. Teaching a general strategy makes more sense than teaching children how to solve specific problems because the same strategy can be applied to a wide variety of situations not only in the classroom but in the world at large.

## Why set problems?

If the problems we set require the children to make choices, then we can be assured that they are thinking for themselves. Making decisions about a solution to a problem is a creative activity and often the end product will be an expression of the child's personality. Furthermore, if the solution works, or is at least partially effective, the child will gain in confidence to tackle further problems. We must therefore use our skill as teachers to set problems that stretch the imagination of the child but at the same time lie within his or her sphere of ability.

Psychological research has shown that youngsters may adopt different approaches to problem solving or, indeed, the process of learning itself. On the one hand, there is the child who prefers to learn step by step in a logical fashion. On the other, there is the child who prefers a process by which an overall view is obtained before he or she chooses a route to understanding. The second of these two children might be described as a creative thinker and it is this kind of person who might find learning science or maths difficult. This difficulty may lie in the step-by-step way in which we teach these subjects rather than in their content. Science-related problem solving can, however, benefit all pupils because it allows both learning strategies to flourish. How many problems do we solve by jumping from one idea to another before the best solution dawns on us? At other times, we might approach the problem more systematically until the solution is achieved.

**10** Skills can be more effectively learnt when children perceive a reason for doing so

Children's personalities cannot be classified with such simple precision — only the extremes have been mentioned here — but is it possible that large numbers of students with creative minds have been lost to the world of science and technology because of our traditional, serialist methods of teaching?

Problem solving activities can provide a situation in which learning many abstract skills becomes more meaningful to children. It makes much more sense to a child to learn how to measure in metres and centimetres through finding the maximum distance a glider can fly. Children learn the social skills of communication, compromise and cooperation when they are involved in a group effort to build a bridge out of straws to span half a metre and support a 100 g mass. Children get a 'feel' for the concept of area if they observe its effect on the fall of a series of different sized paper parachutes. Compare the effectiveness of this with the usual static exercise on area found in a maths book. Both exercises are necessary but practical problem solving is about area with a purpose; area in action.

A number of teachers have commented on an interesting fact when their children have completed a problem solving exercise. Quite often they have been surprised to find that some of their 'less able' children have done particularly well in solving a problem. Of course, the label 'less able' is largely an assessment of children's academic ability and probably throws no light on their ability in other areas. If, then, we are to be fair to all the children in our classes and if we are to give them as broad an education as possible, then practical activities such as problem solving must form a greater part of the curriculum.

## Success and failure

If children are to gain confidence from their practical work, it will be important that they experience a large degree of success especially in the early stages. Failure to solve a problem completely, however, is not a disaster and is an inevitable part of tackling the challenges that face us. Prepare the children for this by telling them not to give up when the going gets rough but you should sometimes be prepared to tell them how to get out of a difficult situation when all else fails.

If we ask children to make, say, a model of a space station using any materials they can find then each will respond at his or her own level. The end product will vary according to the differing abilities in the class. No-one, however, will have failed in their task. There will simply be varying degrees of artistic achievement. On the other hand, if we ask that a working model of a sycamore key (a seed with its wing) be made, then success or failure will be all too apparent. If the model refuses to spin as it descends then quite clearly something is wrong. The child will have to face up to the fact that the problem is not yet solved. She must be encouraged to analyse the situation, decide what is wrong and make adjustments to the model. At some point the child may be tempted to give up and it is this we want to avoid. The teacher will have to decide whether to encourage her to go back and try again on her own, or to solve the problem for her. The answer to the dilemma, of course, lies in knowing the child. How far can she be pushed, with appropriate hints, to work out her own solution? Is she the kind of child that gives up easily?

In holding back information the teacher may find herself acting in an unfamiliar way. We are more used to dispensing knowledge and giving instructions. It almost goes against the grain to suppress information and refuse the help that has been requested and yet this is often necessary in problem solving activities if children are to be encouraged to think for themselves.

Compare these two conversations. Sally is making a sound device.

*Sally:* 'My block of wood makes too much noise when it hits the table. What can I do?'
*Teacher:* 'Why not wrap the block in some cloth? That should do the trick.'

Alternatively a better response from the teacher would have been:

*Teacher:* 'Well, you tell me what might soften the landing of the block.'
*Sally:* 'Could I put newspaper on the desk?'
*Teacher:* 'Yes, that's good, but what else might do the job?'
*Sally:* 'Some cotton wool or some polythene bags.'
*Teacher:* 'That's fine. Is there any thing you could do to the block instead of the table?'

And so on. The teacher will go on to ask a string of questions that would draw from Sally a collection of possible solutions to her immediate problem. Eventually she will choose for herself the idea she thinks will work best.

To a child with more confidence and initiative, the teacher might simply have said: 'I don't really know what you can do but let me know when you have found the answer.' Children may even find it encouraging to be aware that their teacher 'doesn't know' the answer to a particular question. They will certainly delight in telling her as soon as they have found out for themselves!

Early success and encouragement are important, so with this in mind each of the topics that follow begin with easily solved tasks, progressing later to harder ones. At the beginning, at least, the atmosphere should be one of encouragement and praise.

## Boys and girls

Much has been said recently about involving girls more in the scientific and technological aspects of the curriculum. The problem of girls under-achieving in this area seems to become more acute as they grow older. Some teachers in the primary and middle school years might wonder what all the fuss is about if they are lucky enough not to have experienced these problems. Girls' and boys' attitudes, however, are largely influenced by what adults expect of them in these early years, so the correct teacher attitude is important. Equally important is that boys and girls should be able to see women teachers tackling subjects such as heavy crafts and the technological aspects of science.

Boys may have acquired a small advantage over girls when the problems to be solved are centred on devices similar to the kinds of toys that they have been given in the past. On the other hand, generally speaking, girls may have a greater ability to communicate and cooperate in a group as they solve a problem. In the end the wisest thing to do is to assume that you have a unisex class and give each member equal opportunity as well as expecting the best response that each child can offer.

## General organisation

All the projects in this book have been extensively trialled with non-specialist teachers working in a classroom or laboratory. In most cases, all the children in the class have tackled the problem at the same time although it might suit some teachers to arrange smaller groups for such work.

Practical lessons, especially those in which children are constructing different models, with all the decisions and choices this involves, can be hectic. In my experience, children have a lot to talk about and at times the noise level may rise in the room. A quick glance around, however, usually indicates that it is a productive noise level and that all the children are involved in their problem. Much useful discussion will be going on and often there will be movement around the room. For children unused to such activity, a few rules of behaviour stated at the beginning will aid the smooth running of the lesson.

Practical problem solving is the ideal setting in which children can learn to cooperate with each other. It is often extremely important to them that they 'work with their friend'. This desire to work with a partner is to be encouraged though you may decide sometimes to engineer the partnerships yourself. Generally, as the size of the working group increases, the children will need to exercise greater social skills. Also, larger groups may include one or two children who are excluded from the task in hand. If you have large working groups, ensure that the individuals are capable of a fair amount of cooperation and that there is enough within the task to usefully occupy everyone. At times it may be best for children to work individually on a problem. This does not mean, of course, that they stop communicating with and possibly helping each other, but it does ensure that each child is more likely to be actively involved in the work.

To avoid having children waiting for attention, the teacher might consider using cards with 'helpful hints' to which the children can be directed when they encounter difficulties. For instance, when Mr Goodman set his class the task of making a sound device, those who could not get started might have been given access to cards like these:

---

**Elastic bands make sounds**

Hold a thick elastic band between your fingers and ping it.
Now use a thin one.
Now stretch the thin one more and ping it.

THE SOUND THAT YOU MAKE MUST ALWAYS BE THE SAME.

---

**Drop a marble**

Drop a marble on to a board,
                    some cloth,
                    some card.
Drop it from high up and then low down.

HOW WILL YOU ALWAYS MAKE THE SAME SOUND?

---

Another way of helping those who need attention is, in the early stages of a topic, to arrange the children in groups consisting of a mix of more able and less able children. Inevitably the children will prefer their friendship groups but bear in mind the valuable lessons that can be learnt by a partnership of perhaps an academically able child with an 'average' child of superior practical ability.

Organising the classroom or laboratory effectively will free the teacher for the important task of monitoring the various work groups. The children should know where to get materials and simple tools such as scissors for themselves. Safe tools such as pliers or a hole punch (used for file paper) should have a location in the room to which they are returned for others to use. Costly items such as sticky tape should have a restriction set upon them such as 'Use no more than 10 cm of tape without special permission'. The wider the variety of construction materials available the better, though there may be some problems in which the range of materials is restricted on purpose. The lack of certain materials may be likened to the economic restraints put on design technologists by their employers, so do not be flustered by requests for things that you have not got to hand. Simply make this into another problem to be overcome by the child.

## Materials and tools

Some of the more obvious things such as card, glue, plastic bottles and string will already be available for the children to use but you might consider having some of the following ready to hand:

art straws (paper or plastic)
balsa wood scraps
beads
Clingfilm
corks
cotton reels
cotton thread
cotton wool
drawing pins
dressmaking pins
egg boxes
elastic bands
expanded polystyrene
fabrics – assorted
jam jars
kitchen foil
marbles
masking tape
nails – assorted
nuts and bolts – assorted
paper clips
paper fasteners
pebbles of various sizes
pipe cleaners
Plasticine
plastic containers of all descriptions
polythene bags
rubber innertubes (disused)
wire – coat hangers (disused)
        florists wire (easily shaped by hand)
wood off-cuts
wooden dowel rods of various diameters

craft knife (teacher supervision)
gun stapler
hammer
hole punch
pairs of compasses
pliers, including a wire cutter
scissors
stapler
wooden board to act as a 'bread-board' to protect desk surfaces.

## Science principles to have in mind

Each of the following topics contains examples of the kind of science principles that might, incidentally, be discussed during the problem solving work. There may be other principles that have not been noted and some of those mentioned may not come up during the children's work. In any case, these principles should take a back seat to the process of solving problems.

Because we cannot be sure how our children will solve a particular problem, we cannot reliably predict which scientific ideas they will encounter.

For this reason, it would be a mistake to think that we could use open-ended problem solving as a means of teaching the traditional science curriculum. A teacher intent on teaching his or her class a particular idea would have this objective foremost in his or her mind and would be unable to let the children find their own solution to a particular problem. The most straightforward way to teach a group of children an important concept such as the relationship between the length of a vibrating elastic band and the pitch of the note produced is to give them the *same* practical experiences — an idea alien to the problem solving process. If it had been Mr Goodman's intention to teach his children about the sound properties of elastic bands when he asked his class to make a sound device, he would have had to discourage all the other wonderful machines that did not involve elastic bands. The process of practical problem solving, then, should be included alongside the traditional methods for teaching the science curriculum, not as a substitute for them.

## Summing up

Organising practical work in the classroom or laboratory is not easy but the more often it is done the easier it becomes both for the teacher and the children. Each of the following projects sets out to provide a scheme which might last for half a term. Each detailed Unit in the scheme might represent the work of one lesson of an hour or more, unless some research is involved, in which case allow approximately two and a half hours. It is hoped that such explicit 'lesson plans' will help those who are new to problem solving and who want to avoid the usual pitfalls.

Parts of each scheme can be taken in isolation for those who prefer to try a 'one-off' lesson at first. Indeed, an individual challenge from any of the projects might make a useful addition to one of the schemes in current use at your school.

For those who prefer to create their own schemes of work, the projects will serve as an illustration of the principles of practical problem solving which can be adapted to suit the individual teacher and his or her children.

The greatest difficulty in devising problem solving work for children is in choosing an appropriate brief. It must be suitably open-ended to allow the children to be inventive and to avoid producing the 'one correct answer'. It must cater, when appropriate, for mixed-ability grouping by having suitable solutions at varying levels of sophistication. It must be workable within the considerable constraints of the school situation and, finally, the brief must appeal to children and offer them excitement and success. The following projects attempt to satisfy all these criteria.

# 1 Elastic Energy

## Introduction

Energy is a fundamental and central concept in both science and technology. We are dealing with energy changes every moment of our lives and it is easy to take these for granted. Children need to be made aware of how energy can be stored and then controlled for use when needed. Elastic bands store energy when they are stretched or twisted and it is this principle that we use in the following challenges. The children will be asked to store and control this elastic energy in a variety of ways. If you deem it appropriate, they could be encouraged to think how the energy stored in elastic bands changes into other forms such as 'movement', 'raised' and 'heat' energy.

## UNIT 1
### Elastic powered roller

The first four Units in this topic are based on a toy that children used to make with a cotton reel, elastic band and a matchstick. It used to be called a cotton reel tank but we will call it a 'roller' (figure 1).

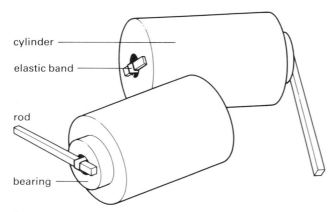

cylinder

elastic band

rod

bearing

**1** The elastic powered roller

One end of the elastic band is anchored to the cylinder while the other end is looped round a rod that is free to rotate when the roller is held in the hand. The toy works by winding the rod round a number of times and then releasing the model to roll along a surface.

## Preliminary discussion

Begin by showing the children the roller you have made and invent names for the various parts. Take each feature (for example, the cylinder) at a time and discuss what else could be used in place of the materials you have introduced.

The cylinder could be

a tin can with a card end
a plastic lemonade bottle
a 35 mm film case
a card tube
two yogurt pots fixed end to end

The bearing could be:

a plastic or wooden bead
a button
a piece of candle wax
a metal washer
a plastic, home-made washer

**2** Various kinds of bearing for the roller

It would be helpful to point out that the elastic band does not have to go through the bearing. It could be fixed to a bent paper clip (figure 3).

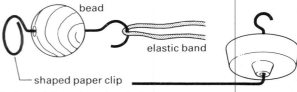

bead

elastic band

shaped paper clip

**3** Attaching the elastic band

The rod could be any one of a variety of things found in the classroom such as a pencil, a piece of stiff card or a length of wire. The length of the rod may be critical but this is for the children to find out in their investigations.

Ordinary classroom elastic bands are suitable but they should be reasonably thick and 5 cm or more in length. It does not matter if the elastic band is loose before it is wound up — it will tighten as it twists — but if the band is tight to start with the rod may jam and prevent it from unwinding.

 *Design and make an elastic band roller. Choose your own materials for the various parts. Try to make yours different from anyone else's.*

It is clear that with so many variations on the design of the roller, the children will have plenty of decisions to make and we should expect to see a wide range of models. You may decide to set the additional challenge that the roller should go as far as possible or as fast as possible. This, of course, will influence the choice of the components that they use.

## Beginning the design process

We are, perhaps, being unfair in asking the children to plunge into this design task without the benefit of preliminary research. Some of the less experienced ones may need time to 'play' with your roller before they decide how to make theirs.

You will need to have time to collect the construction materials and to discuss individual designs with the children. So it is probably wise this time to work through the whole design process, beginning with preliminary drawings.

With this in mind, explain the importance of considering a number of ideas before committing oneself to construction and ask the children briefly to sketch three or four different ideas on paper. The children at this stage are simply toying with the idea of building a roller so the sketches can be done quickly by free hand. Some labelling might be helpful, especially when you come to discuss various points about the model, but this is not essential.

Next, ask the children to choose the most promising of their initial ideas and make a well-labelled design drawing. This time the drawing should stand on its own. It should show all that is necessary for a complete stranger to build the model: the materials that are going to be used, the dimensions of the model and the way in which the components are going to be arranged. Some children might choose to draw more than one view of their model, perhaps a plan view and side elevation.

Leave some time between making these drawings and constructing the models so that either you or the children will be able to gather the necessary bits and pieces that they will need for making the rollers.

## Construction

The construction stage should run smoothly if you have used the children's diagrams to collect tools and materials beforehand. Many useful items can be brought in by the children from home if they have already planned to use them. You will probably need a pair of pliers, and a hammer and a nail for punching holes in tin cans or plastic bottles. If some of your children have chosen the traditional candle wax bearing, then you will need a small saw and something to gouge a hole through the centres of the slices of candle. This can conveniently be done by using a 6 mm (¼ inch) drill bit held in the hand and twisted back and forth until a hole has been worn through (figure 4).

Other possible bearings include bottle tops and home-made plastic washers. If children find it difficult to thread the elastic band through the bearing — or the cylinder itself for that matter — they could use a bent paper clip 'threader' or a loop of sewing thread. But it is best to encourage them to devise these methods themselves rather than tell them.

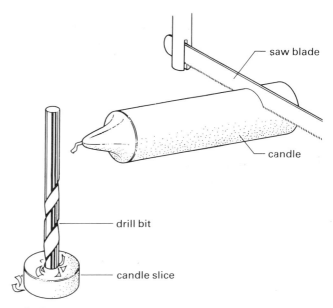

**4** Cutting wax bearings

The elastic bands can be used double, or even treble, if you can spare them. A series of short elastic bands can be looped together to form a longer one to match the length of the cylinder, with very little loss in efficiency.

Finally, arrange the room beforehand so that the children have space to run their models when they are made. Some rollers will only go a few centimetres and these can perform on the desk top, but those made with large cylinders will easily travel the length of the room, so be prepared!

## Putting the roller through its paces

Once the children have made their rollers, they will trial them without having to be asked to. They will make adjustments to improve performance and may even change parts of the original design. However, it would be a good idea to have a worksheet ready to guide them through more structured trials when this initial testing is finished. This has the added advantage of giving you time to attend to those children with difficulties while the more able ones go on.

The worksheet might be designed like the one shown on page 14.

## ELASTIC ENERGY ROLLER

1  Wind up your roller 10 times.
   Let it roll.
2  Wind it up 20 times if you can.
   Let it roll.
   Did it go twice as far the second time? _____
3  Complete this table for your roller.

| Number of winds | 5 | 10 | 15 | 20 | 25 | 30 |
|---|---|---|---|---|---|---|
| Distance travelled (cm) | | | | | | |

   What do you notice about your results?

   _____

4  What kind of slope can your roller climb?_____

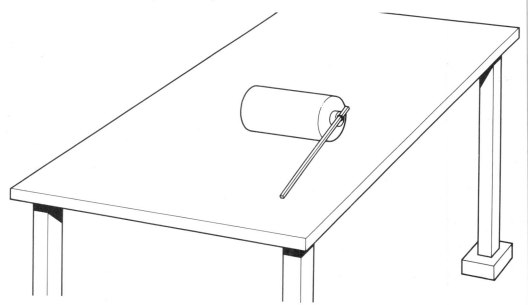

   Find out how many centimetres you can lift one end of your
   desk while your roller continues to climb.
5  Make an obstacle course for your roller out of pieces of card,
   books and pencils and so on.
   What is the highest 'wall' your roller can climb? _____

**5** A wide variety of rollers can be constructed

## Summary

A suitable way to conclude this Unit would be for everyone to watch each roller, operated by its designer, as it clambers over one of the obstacle courses mentioned at the end of the worksheet. Of course, if you have challenged the children to make a high-speed roller then a light-hearted race will enable each member of the class to observe the variety of designs in action. Ask the class to look for the features that make the rollers perform well. Can they analyse the deficiencies in the slower rollers?

---

**SCIENCE PRINCIPLES TO HAVE IN MIND**
The teacher must decide how far to take the discussion of *energy changes* with his or her children and this will depend on their previous experience and level of development.
- **Energy is stored in the elastic band. Where does this energy come from?**
- **The elastic energy changes to 'raised' and 'movement' energy as the roller climbs a slope.**
- **There is a *friction* force between the bearing and the cylinder and also between the rod and the ground. How can this be overcome?**
  If the roller tends to skid on release then there is insufficient friction between the cylinder and the ground.
  These two facts conveniently illustrate both the advantages and disadvantages of friction.
- **How do lubricants work?**
- **How does the bearing work on the roller?**
- **How do bearings work in other vehicles?**
(The area of contact and hence the friction between moving parts is reduced.)

---

## UNIT 2
### Improving the roller

Now that the roller has been made, we have the chance to investigate how we can change its performance by altering some of its features. Suppose we want to design a roller that goes as far as possible for a given number of winds. What can we change to improve its range?

> The bearing?
> The size of the cylinder?
> The length of the rod?
> The number of elastic bands?

If we change all of these variables at once, we will not know which of them has improved the performance of the roller. Therefore, we should proceed scientifically and change only one thing at a time.

The following problem, then, is slightly different from the others in this book. It involves planning and executing an experiment rather than designing and making a working model. The common feature, of course, is that of design where the children have to make decisions for themselves in order to achieve a particular goal.

 *Decide on one change that you can make to your roller to make it roll further. Design and carry out an experiment that tests your idea.*

The children could work individually or in groups on the design of their experiment. A preliminary class discussion will help those with limited experience in experiment design. For example, you might all agree to investigate the effect of increasing the diameter of the roller cylinder. Stress the importance of keeping all the other variables constant. In both trials, we should keep the *same* rod, elastic band and bearing.

An interesting point to note is that in increasing the diameter of the cylinder we will be increasing its mass slightly as well as changing the area of contact with the floor. We can probably ignore these small changes but the problem is worth discussing with the children. (An enterprising child might suggest adding a small piece of Plasticine to the lighter roller to counter the problem of increased mass, in which case it is worth doing.)

Children who have had a lot of experience in designing experiments of their own will be able to cope with this task without too much help. Others, however, may need more guidance, which could be in the form of a worksheet like the one on page 16.

There are various ways of increasing the diameter of a roller. For example, a completely new

# WORKSHEET TWO

## MAKING THE ROLLER GO FURTHER

1 How many winds will you give your roller each time you test it?

2 Draw a diagram to show how you will increase the diameter of your roller.

3 Complete this table for your roller *before* you increase its diameter.

|  | Distance travelled for _____ winds (cm) |
|---|---|
| 1st try |  |
| 2nd try |  |
| 3rd try |  |

4 Increase the diameter of your roller but keep everything else the same if you can.

5 Complete this for your new roller. (Remember to keep the same number of winds.)

|  | Distance travelled (cm) |
|---|---|
| 1st try |  |
| 2nd try |  |
| 3rd try |  |

6 Make changes to the diameter of your roller until you are satisfied that it goes as far as possible. Record your results each time you make a change.

cylinder could be used or a light substance such as foam rubber could be wrapped round the existing cylinder and a new card surface fixed on to this. Probably the best solution, though, is to stick a card disc at each end of the cylinder thus forming larger-diameter 'wheels' (figure 6).

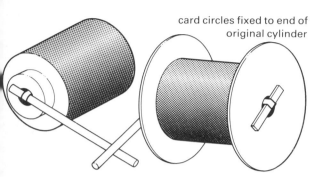

card circles fixed to end of original cylinder

**6** Enlarging the diameter of the roller

You could discuss how to find the average of the three distances on the worksheet or you could simply leave the results as they are presented here. Making a comparison between the two tables should be fairly easy without the additional mathematics.

Are the children clear about why there should be three 'tries' for each roller? (The first try could be a freak and give completely the wrong impression.) For that matter, are the children satisfied that three tries are enough?

Younger children might find that the whole exercise becomes clearer if they make two rollers instead of modifying one. If they make two identical rollers, and then change the diameter of one of them, they can start both together and see immediately which goes further.

## Extension work

Children who finish their experiment involving one change of cylinder diameter should be encouraged to investigate further increases.

Children who get very far ahead can go on to investigate changes in the other components of the roller such as doubling the elastic bands or lubricating the bearing.

## Summary

If the roller diameter is increased too much, the elastic band will not be able to push it along. There is, therefore, an optimum size for any particular roller design which makes it roll as far as possible. The children who can spot this will have done very well. Perhaps the matter can be raised in the class discussion that takes place once the experiments have been carried out.

Can the children identify points of error that will have made their results slightly inaccurate? Have they been entirely fair in their work? Casting doubts on the validity of their results is a healthy exercise worth carrying out now and then.

> **SCIENCE PRINCIPLES TO HAVE IN MIND**
> • **A larger diameter wheel travels further for a single turn than a smaller one. The force required to turn it, however, is greater. This illustrates the fundamental principle behind the working of gears.**
> • **Those investigating the effect of a change in the bearing or the elastic bands will meet the principles of *friction*, *lubrication* and *energy changes*.**

# UNIT 3
## Motorised fan

At the moment, the children will have a wide variety of rollers — some that run sluggishly and others that run rapidly. If the cylinder is held in the hand, the speed at which the rod unwinds will depend largely on the bearing used as well as on the size and twist of the elastic band. The next challenge focuses attention on, amongst other things, the friction between the bearing and the cylinder because the roller is now going to be used as a high-speed motor.

### Preliminary discussion

Ask the children what they think happens inside a hairdryer to cause air to be blown outwards. How does the propeller on an aircraft pull it along? What goes on inside a vacuum cleaner? Have they ever seen a cooling fan? Obviously, if you have pictures, or better still examples, of real fans or propellers, these will be of great assistance.

The children need to realise that two things are required to move air around mechanically: a motor and a fan or propeller. Look closely at the blades of a fan or propeller. How is the air pushed forwards or backwards? The blades have a 'twist' or pitch. What would happen if the pitch was too great or too little? The fact that the sideways movement of the angled fan blade pushes the air forwards is a difficult one for children to appreciate. It all happens so quickly, and of course air is 'invisible'. Ask the children to take a stiff piece of card about A4 size or larger and wave it in the air. If the card is 'flat on' to the air (figure 7a), the children will create plenty of turbulence. If the card is 'edge on' to the direction of movement (figure 7b), it will merely slice through the air and cause very little disturbance. Now ask them to hold the card at an angle as they wave it through the air (figure 7c). They should experience some air movement especially at right angles to the direction of motion of the card.

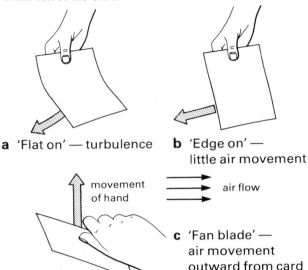

**a** 'Flat on' — turbulence   **b** 'Edge on' — little air movement

movement of hand

air flow

**c** 'Fan blade' — air movement outward from card

**7** Working out the principle of the fan

*Use your roller as a high-speed motor to drive a fan of your own design. Your fan will need to blow as hard as possible and will be tested on a 'blow-meter'.*

Of what materials could we make the fan blades in the classroom? Card, thin plastic, balsa wood? (The plastic from lemonade bottles or ice cream containers is useful because children can cut the shapes they need with scissors.)

How many blades should the fan have and what shape could they be?

What can we fix the blades to? (If the blades are cut out of a single piece of plastic or card then this eliminates the need to fix them to a central hub.)

What problems will we encounter when we fix the blades to the motor?

What kind of bearing will be best to produce high speeds? (Have some beads about the size of a marble ready as these are particularly suitable.)

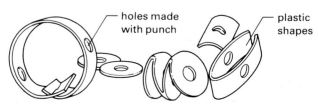

holes made with punch

plastic shapes

**8** Bearings that children could make

Could some enterprising children make their own bearings? (See figure 8.)

Some children might suggest lubricating their own bearings. If you think this is a good idea, have some suitable substances ready such as bicycle lubricating oil, butter or talcum powder.

Will you allow your children one 'standard' elastic band or give them the freedom to choose the type and number they want?

They will find it is quite a simple matter to give their card or plastic blades a small twist or fold. The elastic band may be looped over this kind of blade or fixed in some other way. Some children, however, may wish to fix their flat blades to a hub. This will work as long as the blades can be slotted securely on to the hub. A cork that has been slotted with a sharp knife would be suitable. Plasticine is less satisfactory but has the advantage of being quickly changed by the children when they experiment with the pitch of the blades.

The children will need to realise that if they are to make alterations to their models to improve performance, they will need a reliable test to measure their improvements. They might have some interesting thoughts on the design of a 'blow-meter' or you might decide to present them with a device similar to the one shown in figure 9.

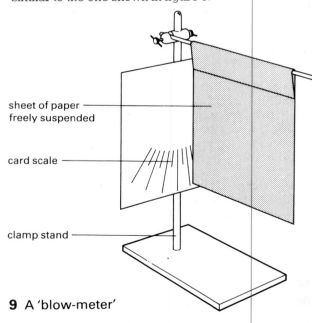

sheet of paper freely suspended

card scale

clamp stand

**9** A 'blow-meter'

While the children solve this design problem they will probably find that if their blades are too large, they will not be able to spin fast enough; and if they are too small, they will not shift enough air. The pitch of the blades is also critical. If there is too much twist the air will slow down the blades and too little will result in a diminished air flow.

**10** Measuring the 'blowing power' of a fan

## Summary

Success in the exercise depends on finding a careful balance between all the factors involved and choosing materials that are strong enough to withstand rough treatment. When the children have the chance to watch each other's models in action, can they spot any common features in those that work well? Can they appreciate the concept of optimum conditions that are necessary for the best performance?

> **SCIENCE PRINCIPLES TO HAVE IN MIND**
> ● **Bearings and lubrication are necessary for high-speed movement.**
> ● **The principle of the fan (closely related to that of the aircraft propeller and the ship's screw).**
> ● **The idea of *optimum conditions* for a device to work well. (Compare with the tuning of a car engine.)**

# UNIT 4
## Motor-driven toy

To complete the work on rollers, we can set the children an open-ended design problem in which their roller drives a 'toy' of their choice.

*Design and make a toy which is driven by an elastic-band roller. Your toy should have a slowly rotating part.*

The children will know by now that they can achieve a slow rotation by using a candle wax bearing. Have some spare candles ready because a few bearings may break. (For this reason, it is probably worth teaching the children how to make their own. See figure 4.)

What kinds of 'toy' have rotating parts? The list is endless: windmill, clock, helicopter, merry-go-round, record player and so on. One class of children I know decided to make an entire fair ground with each child contributing a model.

The whole design process from doodles to final plans on paper, then construction, testing and improvements can be encompassed in this project. The children will need to decide before they make their design drawing how they will harness the energy in their elastic bands and how they will make their models attractive as well as functional. These are all the problems of the design technologist.

You might decide to supply each child or team of children with a plastic cotton reel or, alternatively, you could give them the added challenge of devising their own cylinder inside their model. Of course, a 'cylinder' is not really necessary. What is required is an anchor point for one end of the elastic band and a surface on which the bearings can run. These features can be provided by an ordinary box or a U-shaped length of stiff wire (figure 11).

bearing fitted at this end ———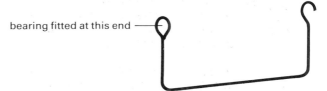

**11** A U-shaped piece of wire is sufficient to support the elastic band motor

If a workshop is available so that wood can be cut, drilled and shaped, then that is a bonus. But most models can be made out of stiff card, plastic containers and wire in the classroom or laboratory.

Since the children have done a lot of work with the roller as a vehicle, they may be tempted to construct a moving car or lorry to fulfil this brief. This could present a number of technical problems that the children, unless particularly able, will not be able to overcome. So it is advisable to dissuade anyone from doing this. If you are keen to let your children design four-wheeled vehicles driven by elastic bands, then refer to the buggy described in Chapter 4 (page 46).

## Summary

In this project, the children are learning that sources of energy have to be harnessed and controlled if they are to be of use to people. It requires a large leap of the imagination from the desk top to, for example, the internal workings of a hydroelectric power station but the technological principles are the same.

**12** 'Toys' worked by an elastic band motor

## UNIT 5
### Paddle boat

If you have a large sink, a long plastic plant trough or even a child's paddling pool at your disposal, you can consider the construction of elastic-powered paddle boats.

As in many of the problems in this book, the following challenge presents the children with a situation in which many of the awkward decisions have been made but those remaining are varied and challenging enough for a mixed-ability class.

A simple design for a paddle boat hull is shown to the children (figure 13) and their attention is focused on the design of the paddle and the way in which the boat is propelled.

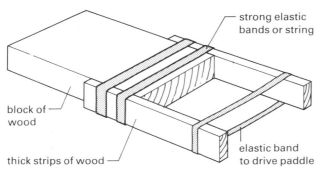

block of wood

thick strips of wood

strong elastic bands or string

elastic band to drive paddle

**13** An easily constructed paddle-boat hull

A boat like this can be made out of almost anything. For instance, a squeezy bottle with two pencils tied on would work just as well.

*Design and make a paddle that will fit into the elastic band at the back of the paddle boat. The paddle should propel the boat forward as far as possible.*

Give all the children one 'standard' elastic band and explain that if their boats reach the end of the 'boating lake', they can be turned round immediately to continue on their journeys.

The children will need to consider the following:

The use of waterproof material for the paddle; for example, plastic or thin pieces of wood.
The shape the blades should be.
The number of blades that will be necessary.

An important point to notice is that, while a wide blade will give more push through the water, it will also prevent the elastic band from winding up as much as it could do, and the twisted elastic might jam the blade (figure 14). With thoughtful paddle design, this problem can be overcome and the efficiency of the blade increased.

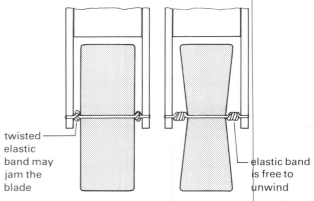

twisted elastic band may jam the blade

elastic band is free to unwind

**14** Creating an efficient paddle

Once again, the type of plastic found in cartons and bottles of all descriptions is very suitable for the construction of the paddle. In most cases, the children can cut it with a simple pair of scissors and it can often be folded into shape. Polystyrene meat trays also provide an excellent material. The children might even choose to use the curved edge of these trays to make their paddles more efficient.

Paddles with more than two arms can be easily made by slotting blades together to form a four-arm paddle. Plastic is difficult to glue unless the correct type of glue is used, so encourage the children to fix plastic bits together by using slots or staples.

### Extension work

The children can never really finish an investigation like this because there are so many possible solutions to the problem. If they do require further stimulus, however, set them the task of devising steering mechanisms for their paddle steamers.

Teachers with access to woodwork tools might like to take this project further by introducing a challenge based on the best design for the paddle-boat hull. The children could cut their own hull shapes from pieces of softwood and perhaps, later, add a funnel and passenger accommodation.

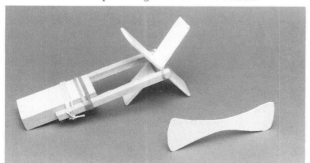

**15** The paddle boat with two possible paddle designs

## Summary

When the work is finished, ask the children to watch each other's models.

Which work best?
Which boats, rather than going the furthest, go the fastest?
What are the common features of the best paddles?

The ability to generalise about the paddle designs is an important scientific skill to foster in the children. Could it be that the paddles with the largest surface area work the best? Or do the paddles that allow the greatest number of winds of the elastic band have the best performances? Possibly those blades that have a cupped shape are superior to those that are flat.

Following this summing up session, you might ask the children to record how they would make an improved paddle. Their drawings and comments would provide a useful assessment of their ability to learn from practical experience.

> **SCIENCE PRINCIPLES TO HAVE IN MIND**
> ● **How can we achieve the maximum energy output from the elastic band?**
> ● **What forces act on the boat while it is in motion?**
> ● **Does the water get pushed backwards while the boat goes forwards? (Action and reaction.)**

## UNIT 6
### Bottle boat

While you still have the paddling pool out, try this further twist in the tale of the elastic band. The idea began where most of the ideas in this book began — under a hot shower — and this explains why it centres on a discarded shampoo bottle, though any old plastic bottle will do.

This last elastic project is really only suitable for a small group of children because they may need help with certain aspects of the construction. Children will be excited by the boat design but a certain amount of preparation is required by the teacher. The boat is driven by a submerged propeller which will probably turn out to be similar in design to the fan that the children made in Unit 3 but smaller. Once again, the children are given the basic hull arrangement and asked to experiment with the method of propulsion.

### The hull

The hull could be a shaped piece of wood but it adds interest to make this out of a discarded plastic bottle. This naturally reduces preparation time as well as cost. Shampoo bottles are particularly good because of their almost boat-like shape to begin with — though this might require a small stretch of the imagination! An important feature of the hull is the 'bracket' that holds the rotating propeller. This needs to be made out of fairly thin wire with the aid of a pair of pliers. It screws on to the bottle by using the cap, as shown in figure 16.

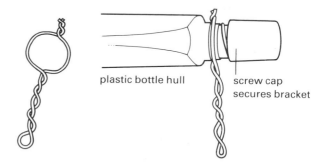

plastic bottle hull     screw cap
secures bracket

**16** The wire bracket

The children could make this component if suitable wire is chosen. It should be strong enough to resist the tension in the twisted elastic band yet malleable enough to be shaped by young hands.

### The motor and propeller

The propeller must be fixed on to a similar length of wire which can be shaped as shown in figure 17.

This end of the shaft should be coiled like a spring so that the propeller can be conveniently slotted between the coils. Make sure the straight shaft meets the centre of the blades.

**17** The wire shaft

The hook takes one end of the elastic band while the twist will allow a plastic propeller to be slipped in and out fairly easily. This wire shaft could be made by the children by shaping a paper clip with a pair of pliers. The complete arrangement is shown in figure 18.

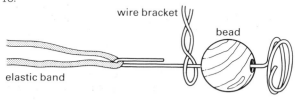

wire bracket

bead

elastic band

**18** The shaft and bearing mounted in the bracket

The other end of the elastic band is attached to another paper clip that hooks on to the front of the boat. The small hole for this clip can be made with a compass point and should be on the top of the boat to keep the hull watertight (figure 19).

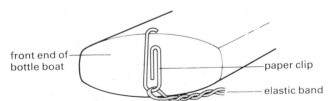

front end of bottle boat

paper clip

elastic band

**19** Fixing the elastic band at the bow

Once the children have overcome the problems of building the boat, they will be able to test a variety of propellers cut out of plastic from containers. The challenge could be as follows:

CHALLENGE 6

*Make a propeller for your boat that takes it as far as possible for 20 winds.*

You can change the challenge to make it a speed test and have a race but the race will probably be over in a few seconds and worse still the boat may not be strong enough to stand up to the rigours of speed boating. You will also need more space in the water for a competitive race involving more than one boat whereas distance trials can be performed in a large sink with the single boat being turned round when it reaches the side.

If the blades are given quite a large twist then the

propellers will work well. If it is difficult to twist the blades then folding will also do the trick. Unless the bead used as a bearing is particularly large, the propeller may not clear the end of the bottle cap and so the propeller size will be limited. This also depends on the length of the wire bracket described at the beginning of this section.

An interesting variation on twisting the blades from a piece of plastic would be to use a cork with a straight shaft skewered into it. Slots could be cut in the cork at appropriate angles and blades of plastic or thin pieces of balsa wood could be fixed into these (figure 20).

If the wire shaft can be pushed all the way through the cork and bent round at the end, it will prevent the blade arrangement swivelling round as the motor turns.

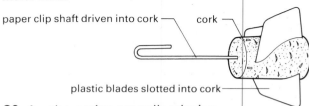

paper clip shaft driven into cork

cork

plastic blades slotted into cork

**20** An alternative propeller design

## Summary

Many of the problems met in this stage, besides those of finding a suitable propeller arrangement, will be concerned with getting the mechanism to spin smoothly. However, even an inefficient arrangement that spins only a few times or unwinds intermittently will propel the boat a little way and provide encouragement for further investigation.

Finally, an interesting feature of this boat, if a flat bottle has been used, is that it may be possible to turn it upside down, wind up the propeller and see it move through the water as a flying boat or a hovercraft. But that is another investigation to be saved for another day!

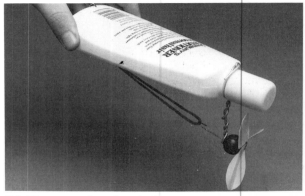

**21** The complete bottle boat

# 2 Seeds on the Move

## Introduction

Being observant is an extremely valuable skill to be encouraged in all aspects of a child's school work. Observing all kinds of natural phenomena stands at the beginning of the science process. Without using our senses to notice the world around us, how can we question what we see and devise experiments to find the answers?

But how do we teach children to be observant? Is simply sitting and looking enough? Usually we expect children to respond to their subject by drawing, writing or talking about what they see. Certainly observation should be an active rather than a passive pursuit. There are, in fact, many different techniques to aid the skill of observation. For instance, ask a child to make up a questionnaire about his or her subject and then fill in his or her own answers. Useful questions might include: How long? How many? What will happen if . . .? Why is it that shape? Give the child a card 'window' through which he or she can observe and draw only parts of the whole. This might be especially useful when there is too much to take in all at once, such as on a visit to a building site or when observing a large potted plant. Attention can be focused on parts of a complex subject by using a camera. After all, what is a photograph but a window on the world?

An observing activity that is extremely worthwhile is that of model making. How much more will a child learn about an insect or a crystal if he or she has to make a scale model of it based on observations? If, in addition, the model has to function in some way, then the observations will need to be even more profound.

This topic on travelling seeds is designed to encourage close observation of natural forms and the way they behave by challenging the children to build working models of seeds and their modes of dispersal. The research beforehand can involve sketching, asking questions and watching the behaviour of the seeds as they move. The model making will involve planning, making, testing, and improving. The children will have to select appropriate materials of construction and decide how best to test their models.

The need for seed dispersal can be referred to constantly throughout this topic and will take on greater meaning as the children see their models 'disperse'.

While observation is important in this topic, the children will also need to appreciate properties of materials such as lightness, rigidity and strength.

The topic continues to build confidence in decision making and problem solving.

## UNIT 1 (Part 1)
### Sycamore keys

One of the most easily obtainable winged fruits is that of the sycamore. We are all familiar with the spinning action of the seeds and undoubtedly children have played with them with interest and delight. They are available all the year round either on the trees in early summer or scattered on the ground for the rest of the year. They can be collected as they fall green and fresh from the trees in summer and autumn and allowed to dry to a crisp brown to be stored for future use. Although the seeds and their wings grow in pairs on the tree, they only spin properly as a single unit. Show some of these to the children and suggest that they try to build a large working model of one.

*Find out how your sycamore key spins through the air. Then make a working model of it at least 10 cm long.*

### Research

Naturally, before children can make an enlarged copy of the key, they will need to look closely at the way it is made and the way it behaves. Can they identify different parts of the key: the seed, the wing, the stiff spine and so on? (See figure 1.)

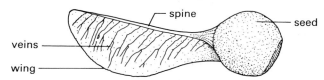

**1** Naming the parts of the sycamore key

Children will enjoy inventing their own names for these parts. What is the average length of the keys you have collected? How much of the length is wing and how much is seed? How much variation is there in shape and colour? Where does the key 'balance' on a ruler edge? Use a lens to make a sketch of the veins on the wing or sketch a series of keys with differing shapes.

Now how does the key fly? Hold the key in different positions and drop it. Does it always spin in the same way or are some starting positions better than others? There is one position from which the key will not spin. Can the children discover this? What happens when you try to throw the key up? How high can you throw it? Outside on a windy day, how far sideways can your key fly? Could you possibly simulate a strong wind in the classroom by using a large cooling fan? Drop the keys in front of this and see how far they travel.

Questions like these will focus the attention of the child on various aspects of the flight of the key and could usefully be arranged on a worksheet. Attention could be drawn to the number of spins the key makes during a descent of, say, one metre. Does the key always spin clockwise or anticlockwise and is this the same for all keys? From which height must the key be dropped to achieve a single rotation? And so on. The list of investigative questions is endless. All will help to give the children an intuitive understanding of the flight of their keys.

This research stage could now be usefully extended to a study of other seeds dispersed by spinners. Are the children aware that the sycamore is related to the Norway maple and field maple and that these trees have similar but differently shaped keys?

Just as intriguing, probably because they are not so apparent, are the small winged seeds that are found tucked inside the cones of many coniferous trees (figure 2). These vary in shape and size and may not possess a stiff spine. Their wings are often paper thin, making them harder to handle without damage.

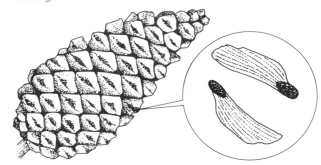

**2** The winged seeds from a Scots pine cone

Take a mature cone from a conifer such as Norway spruce (Christmas tree), larch, cedar or Scots pine and tap it upside down on a hard surface. If you are lucky, a number of wings will be shaken free. If you peel back the protective 'teeth' of the cone, you may be able to dislodge more of them with your fingers or even pull some out with a pair of tweezers. The children will be interested to see the similarities between the conifer seeds and the sycamore keys and may use the information gained in their spinner design.

## UNIT 1 *(Part 2)*
### *Making models of sycamore keys*

When the children have become familiar with the flight of the spinners and have noted as many things

as they can about their form and structure, they will be well prepared to tackle the problem of how to make an enlarged, working model of a sycamore key. First the materials of construction must be chosen:

What can we use for the wing? (Tissue paper, aluminium foil, net curtain, cellophane . . .?)
What will take the place of the seed? (Plasticine, thick card, a button, a coil of wire . . .?)
Should we use a spine and if so what should this be?

As always, encourage the children to find their own materials instead of copying someone else's choice.

Besides choosing their materials, the children will need to spend some of their time testing their models and altering them until they work. They will probably need to stand on their desks to drop their models. (Shoes off and warn the Head!) Not all arrangements will be successful — the working model demands a careful balance of mass and area. Warn the children that they will have to persevere to achieve satisfactory results. They should work towards making their model as light as possible and making it spin as many times as possible.

**3** A collection of sycamore seed models

### Extension work

This kind of open-ended problem could quite obviously go on for ever. There are always improvements to be made and there are always different combinations of materials to use. For those who need an extra challenge, however, ask them to make a spinning model of their own design that has two wings.

### A model guaranteed to work

If you feel this is necessary after the children have made their own models, you could show them one method that produces a satisfactory result (figure 4). Also, if you have this one in mind as the children create their own inventions, you may be able to give the one small hint that will tip the balance between success and failure for some of them.

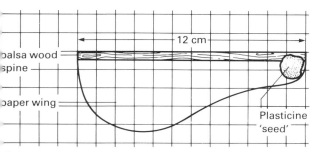

**4** Blueprint for a model sycamore key

## Summary

Naturally, children will want to see what other groups in the room have achieved, especially if their invention has not worked too well. Get the children to describe the flight of each spinner as its designer releases it. Sometimes this verbal description helps in the analysis the children must make if they are to improve a model's performance.

This would be a good time to ask the children why they think seeds need to 'fly'.

**SCIENCE PRINCIPLES TO HAVE IN MIND**
● **The relationship between surface area and *air resistance* will be met. The children should realise that the area is only effective when it is 'facing' the direction of movement.**
● **This would be a good time to discuss the methods by which plants survive to the next generation. Why, for instance, does the sycamore tree produce so many seeds and go to so much trouble to disperse them?**

## Other winged seeds

On completion of Challenge 1 the children might be interested enough to investigate other winged seeds in the same way.

The ash produces a winged key that looks somewhat similar to that of the sycamore but is sufficiently different to warrant an investigation. An excellent way to improve your children's observation would be to ask them to compare the

two types of key. What are their similarities and how do they differ? An ash key (figure 5) seems to have a twist that is necessary for its flight while its seed is perhaps smaller than that of the sycamore.

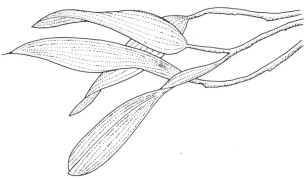

**5** Ash keys

The fruit of the elm contains a small seed the size of a grape pip, surrounded by a paper-thin wing (figure 6). It tends to flutter rather than spin but may be worthy of investigation at this stage. The children's models would need to be fairly small and it would help if they could be released from a high point such as the top of some stairs.

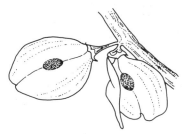

**6** The winged fruit of the elm

It is not certain how much the seed of the lime tree depends on its 'parachute' to escape from the parent tree, but the children may be interested to see this different arrangement (figure 7) and may

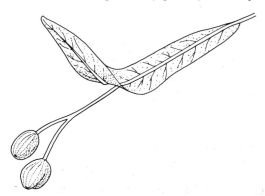

**7** The fruit of the lime

enjoy making a working model. Parachutes, however, are the subject of the next challenge, so perhaps you should delay the introduction of this particular travelling seed.

## UNIT 2 *(Part 1)*
### *Parachutes*

Putting wings on your seeds is one way of sending them abroad but there are other ploys used by the plant kingdom to disperse seeds. Parachutes and similar devices that catch the wind are employed by such plants as the dandelion, rosebay willow-herb and the common sowthistle to name but a few. These parachutes have an array of fine, silken filaments which, when the seed is ripe, catch in the wind and can carry it miles away over land or water. The flying seeds that we used to call 'fairies' in our youth are dispersed by the thistle family and are not really parachute-shaped: the seed is surrounded by a sphere of white hairs which bear it aloft. True parachutes come from goat's beard, ragwort and even some trees such as the London plane but the principle of flight is the same: to catch the wind when the time is ripe and sail away.

The next challenge centres on seeds that are carried on parachutes and since the dandelion is the most common and can be collected almost all the year round, we will use this to begin our investigation. Once again a problem is set and before the children get to grips with it they are encouraged to research the subject by observing the structure and the performance of the seed closely.

 *Make a parachute that will carry a wheat seed to the ground as slowly as possible.*

The fact that a wheat seed (or something similar such as a grain of rice) is specified means that an enlarged parachute must be constructed to carry it. This will be easier to handle than the tiny dandelion seed but inevitably the children's models will fall slightly faster than the real thing.

### How does the dandelion do it?

Since the dandelion parachute is so small, hand lenses and even microscopes should be employed in the initial 'looking' stage. Can the children find the tiny 'hooks' on the seed itself that enable it to anchor to its new home when it arrives there? How are the hairs arranged to form the parachute? Are they just spikes or are there hairs on hairs? Can the children

estimate the lengths of these hairs and the 'stalk' in millimetres? Draw the parachute from above as well as from the side. Get the children to swop their seeds around. Are they all about the same size or do they vary? An experienced group of children will be able to find more questions like these to ask themselves as they look more and more closely at their specimens.

The following activities and questions will help the children to find out how their dandelion parachute works so successfully. Have a few parachutes for each child to use.

Drop your parachute from head height. Does it fall straight down or move sideways a little?
Drop the parachute from an upside-down position. What happens and why?
Let two parachutes go at once. Do they reach the ground together?
Carefully cut some of the hairs from one of the parachutes then drop them both again. What happens this time?
Cut off more hairs and try again.
Cut off all the hairs and watch the difference in the speed of descent.
Cut off the seed from one complete parachute. Let the stalk and hairs drop and describe what happens.
Add a small piece of Plasticine to the seedless parachute until it flies properly again.
Cut a small piece of sticky tape to just cover the top of a complete parachute. Let it drop and see what happens.
Can you say why the dandelion parachute has hairs instead of a canopy like a parachute for humans?
Make the hairs of another parachute wet and then let it fall. Does the water prevent it from 'flying'? If so, why?
Do you ever see seed parachutes 'flying' on a wet day?

While the children answer the questions and make their observations, they will be thinking about the problem they have in hand and possibly making intuitive decisions about its solution.

## UNIT 2 *(Part 2)*
### *Making the model parachute*

During the previous research, you will have discussed suitable names for the various parts of the dandelion fruit such as 'the seed', 'the stalk' and 'the parachute'. The children must now decide how to make these parts and from which materials. Cotton wool is a favourite because it resembles the white hairs of the original parachute, especially if a small piece of it is teased out to make a light ball about the size of a tennis ball. The children know that tissue paper is light so they often choose this for a canopy somewhat like an umbrella. Sometimes aluminium foil is chosen — possibly because it is thin but, I also suspect, just because it looks good! Polythene or cellophane is popular. Do some children see an association between transparency and lightness?

Most children choose to simulate the stalk of the dandelion parachute with a *single* matchstick or piece of thread, but more than one connector could legitimately be used as in a parachute for humans. Children will find that they will have to experiment with the length of this stalk in order to achieve a stable flight — too short and the parachute may topple over; too long and the model will be too heavy.

The most interesting problem the children will have to overcome is that of ensuring a stable descent. If the air trapped under the parachute is unable to escape easily, the model will tip over or sway erratically from side to side. This problem is overcome in the dandelion parachute by the air passing through the hairs as it descends and in a person's parachute by holes in the top of the canopy. If the children have not discovered this yet, then it is something they can establish for themselves during the initial trials of their model. One child solved this problem once without realising why she had done so. She used a floppy piece of polythene as the parachute and curled up the edges, thus allowing the air to escape as her model descended. This inadvertent discovery of a scientific principle often occurs in problem solving and it is one of the important tasks of the teacher to be on hand to take the child that little bit further in his or her understanding.

**8** Models of dandelion 'parachutes'

## Extension work

Ask those who are satisfied that they have solved the parachute problem to modify their device so that it

descends on a sideways slope when dropped from, say, two metres. This might be achieved in a number of ways, such as adding flaps to the parachute or perhaps altering the centre of gravity of the whole model. What kind of plant might the children expect to produce such a sideways-falling seed? Answer: a tall shrub growing away from water in a windless region uninhabited by animals that might otherwise disperse its seeds!

## Summary

It would be a mistake to try to time the descent of the model parachutes because, unless you can arrange to have them released from a high point, such as the top of some stairs, the time span will be too small. A better idea would be to 'race' the models within a group by releasing them at the same time and then 'race' the winners. Alternatively, you may not find it necessary to have any kind of competition at all. The children will have had enough to interest them in constructing and testing their models. They will, however, gain a lot by watching and talking about each other's inventions as each one is demonstrated. Those who have not had time to develop their models to the peak of perfection could easily continue at home. They could demonstrate any significant advances that they have made at a later date.

**SCIENCE PRINCIPLES TO HAVE IN MIND**
- **The idea of releasing air from under the parachute has been mentioned. You might like to discuss the pressure increase that must occur under the canopy.**
- **Surface area versus additional mass will be encountered, as it was in the sycamore challenge. The concept of *air resistance* can be discussed at the appropriate moment.**
- **Possibly the concept of the *density* of materials could be introduced when discussing suitable fabrics for the parachute. If we compare aluminium foil with paper of equal thickness and area, which will be heavier? An electronic balance will be helpful in such a debate.**

## Parachutes in water

If air, in many ways, behaves like a liquid, then why not use a liquid as a slow-motion substitute for air? Teachers who like a touch of the bizarre might like to look into the possibility of presenting a group of children with this challenge.

Make a parachute out of aluminium foil and thin

wire which is similar to a dandelion parachute and carries a small ball of Plasticine. It must descend as slowly as possible through water.

The Plasticine could be about 4 mm in diameter. Make it clear to the children that the aluminium foil will sink in water and give them a thin piece of fuse wire to act as the stalk. Stipulate that no air must be trapped anywhere in the model so that the analogy with the heavier-than-air dandelion parachute is complete. Children will find it instructive to compare the descent of a ball of Plasticine with and without a parachute attached.

## UNIT 3
### Experiments with toy parachutes

An appropriate way to follow the last Unit would be to show your children how to make a simple toy parachute and then ask them to investigate its properties. The parachute should be purposely inefficient so that later the children can make improvements. Use a 20 cm square of fairly thick polythene from a carrier bag. Support a 10 g mass on four lengths of string tied to the corners of the square (figure 9).

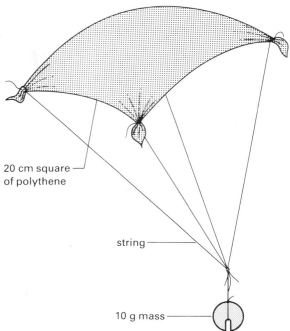

20 cm square of polythene

string

10 g mass

**9** A toy parachute

The children should begin by making a parachute like this for themselves. The parachute should work but not too well. It could be thrown up in a bundle, and should float gently to the ground, or a child could

stand on a desk and release it in an opened position. Ask the children what they could change on the parachute to alter its performance. These suggestions might include changes that speed the descent of the parachute as well as those which slow it down.

Use a lighter or heavier mass.
Use sewing thread in place of the string.
Lengthen or shorten the threads.
Change the shape of the polythene.
Change the area of the polythene.
Use thinner polythene or another material in its place.
Cut holes in the parachute.
Hang the mass off centre.

Next ask the children which of these variables they think will actually slow the descent of the parachute. Once these have been established, set them the next challenge which is one of experiment design rather than model design.

 *Choose one thing that you could change on your first parachute that will make it fall more slowly. Design an experiment to find out if this alteration works.*

The first parachute can serve as a direct comparison with the new, improved ones. If they are dropped simultaneously, then no timing devices will be required.

A worksheet such as the one on page 29 would help children through the decision making process.

This is a good opportunity to discuss with your children why only one variable should be changed in their experiment. If, for instance, they decided to increase the area of the parachute and use a different fabric at the same time, and this resulted in a slowing of the parachute's fall, could they say which of the changes had caused the desired effect?

One group of children I know decided to increase the area of the bin-liner polythene they were using. Having started with a 20 cm square supporting a 10 g mass, they went on to construct squares of 30, 40 and 50 cm. So that they could keep the same length of thread each time, they had to use pieces long enough for the largest of the parachutes. Eventually they found that once the parachute becomes too large in area, it becomes unstable and tips over as it descends.

### Summary

The experiment just described is a very controlled one. We could simply have asked the children to find out how to make the best parachute to carry 10 g. Intuition would have been the children's guide

## MAKING A BETTER PARACHUTE

1  Watch your parachute as it falls. Try it a number of times.
2  Decide to change *one* thing on your parachute to make it fall more slowly.
   Complete: I will change _____
3  Draw a picture to show the one change you will make to your parachute.

4  Make a *new* parachute with the change you have chosen.
5  Ask a friend to help you drop both parachutes at the same time. Do this at least three times.
6  Fill in this table.
   Tick the slower parachute each time.

|  | First parachute | Changed parachute |
|---|---|---|
| 1st try |  |  |
| 2nd try |  |  |
| 3rd try |  |  |

7  Make another parachute with a further change and test it in the same way. (For example, if you have already decreased the size of the mass then decrease it further.)
8  Which of your parachutes worked best and why?

_____

_____

_____

_____

and possibly some clever solutions would have been found. Perhaps as a conclusion to this Unit the children should pool their results and be given time to experiment freely with any parachute design that they choose. They can learn much from each other's work and should be given the opportunity to apply these findings to a free design of their own choice.

> **SCIENCE PRINCIPLES TO HAVE IN MIND**
> If their parachutes tip over, the children will be confronted with the concept of *stability*. Basically, if the *centre of gravity* is below the point of support of a suspended body, the body will be stable and not tip over. The parachute is, of course, supported by air inside the canopy. The lower the mass hangs, the more stable the canopy will be. Compare this with a metre ruler pivoted at its centre. If a lump of Plasticine is fixed below the pivot, the ruler will be stable. If the Plasticine is fixed above the centre, the ruler will swing round.

# UNIT 4
## *Explosive seeds*

Not all seeds that travel through the air sail with the serenity of the dandelion parachute or the grace of the sycamore key. Some, like those of the poppy, are shaken away from the parent plant by devices resembling pepper pots and others, such as broom and vetch, send their seeds off more dramatically with the aid of explosive seed pods. On a warm summer's day, if you are in the vicinity of a gorse or broom bush, you will hear the faint click of the dried, brown pods as they flick open and scatter their seeds.

The next challenge is based on this clever method of seed dispersal. Try to collect some examples of dried seed pods that have not opened. If this is difficult, a film strip or slide strip would be a good substitute. It is not essential that the children see a pod in action but they should understand the principle involved.

*Make a 'seed' by screwing up tightly a 1 cm square of graph paper. Make a device similar to that of a broom pod that will project this 'seed' as far away as possible. Your device should not be more than 10 cm long and will probably look like a simple catapult.*

This limitation on the size of both the 'seed' and the catapult will make the exercise safe enough for the classroom or laboratory. The phrase 'similar to a broom pod' means that children cannot use elastic bands but should think in terms of a springy material that bends and then flicks the 'seed' aloft. It is important to put these restrictions on the children's design for safety reasons. They will have plenty to think about within the confines of the brief.

The catapult will need a base. This could be thick card, a block of wood or something similar. If you provide each team of children with a wooden block to begin with, they can quite easily glue or pin their catapult to it. Drawing pins, paper clips and possibly a gun stapler will all be helpful.

What will the springy part be made from? Many kinds of plastic from containers are suitable, or perhaps a piece of card will do. A thin strip of wood might work or some strips of thin metal such as those found on discarded flat batteries. A school eraser or rubber tubing might well form part of a successful design.

> How many strips and what shape should they be?
> What will hold the 'seed' before it is released?
> At what angle should it be projected from a table top to achieve the maximum range?
> Could children build an adjustable angling device so that the best arrangement can be found during trials?
> Is a trigger necessary for consistent results?

Your children will need to trial their devices, so arrange to have space available for this. Encourage them to give each particular device a fair number of trials and to be analytical in their observations. They should be expected to test, modify and test again as many times as necessary.

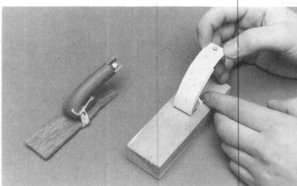

**10** Seed dispersal by catapult

### Extension work

Ask those who need that extra challenge to combine the merits of the broom pod and the sycamore key and make a seed dispersal device that uses both. Can this synthetic seed be projected from a table top to float gently to the ground, or be carried even further on an artificial air current?

> **SCIENCE PRINCIPLES TO HAVE IN MIND**
> • **In perfect conditions, a projectile needs to be launched at 45 degrees to the horizontal in order to go the greatest distance. Can your children come close to finding this out for themselves?**
> • **If the paper 'seed' is not a tight bundle, then its air resistance may slow it down (a point worth discussing as you visit each working group). Do the children know that the dimples on the outside of a golf ball help it to slide further through the air?**

# UNIT 5
## Hanging on

To complete these investigations of the dispersal mechanisms of seeds, we should look at hooked fruits and seeds such as those of great burdock and goose grass. The seed heads of goose grass have many tiny hooks and are most commonly found stuck on or, more painfully, inside the socks of country walkers. The seeds, of course, were originally designed to become attached to animal coats long before woolly jumpers and socks came on the scene. Then, once the tiny hooks had dried sufficiently, the seed would detach itself and, with luck, start a new life well away from the parent plant. If you can collect some of these fascinating seeds or show your children pictures of them, you can present an interesting problem to be solved by the class.

*Make a model of a hooked seed that will attach itself to a woollen sweater hung vertically over the back of a chair. Your 'seed' must be thrown at the sweater from a distance of 1 m and hang on without any extra help.*

The model can be any size the children choose but, of course, if it is too heavy it will not stay attached to a vertical surface.

## Research

The children will benefit if they research the subject first. Use lenses and microscopes to look at the small hooks on the seed cases. Those of the burdock

family can be seen with the naked eye so use these if you can. If you are using goose grass look also at the hairs on the stem. These are used to support the plant as it climbs in its search for light. These hairs are more like downward pointing barbs which catch when pulled in one direction but not in the other. If the children are familiar with the barb on a fishing hook, this may be of use in solving the current problem. So mention this to them. During their observations the children will also note that the hooks on the seed cases are arranged into a ball so that they will be certain to attach to the unsuspecting passer-by no matter from which direction he or she approaches.

## The model

Children may be at a loss as to what materials to use to make their hooks. They may also mistakenly assume that the hooks have to look exactly like the original ones. In fact, any arrangement that catches on to the tiny filaments of wool will suffice, and thin plastic is probably the easiest material to work with in the classroom. A notch in a piece of plastic or even thick paper will quite easily catch the surface of the wool. Alternatively, a pointed spike can be carefully

**11a** A 'notch' cut in thin plastic from a container will make a good hook

**11b** Alternative ways of making hooks in card, plastic or paper

bent over to form the hook. Incidentally, the soft plastic from a yogurt pot can be carefully cut into fine strands that conveniently curl round to form hook-like structures all on their own (figure 11).

Aluminium foil may be chosen as suitable material but can be difficult to cut accurately and is perhaps not rigid enough. Thin copper wire, such as is found in household electrical wiring, could be meticulously shaped by hand to form many-hooked filaments by those who have the patience. Cocktail sticks or used matchsticks could have a notch cut in them with a sharp knife if your children can use one safely.

Having overcome the problem of producing hooked ends to their spikes, the children will have to

**12** Two models of hooked seeds with the seed heads from the great burdock

think of a way of arranging these into a ball. This should not be too difficult for hardened problem solvers as long as they do not make their models too heavy.

## Extension work

Ask particularly able children who need extending to devise a strength test for the models produced in the classroom. This would involve something like loading the model as it hung on the woollen to see what mass it could support. Naturally the test would need to be applied a number of times for each model and an average load value obtained. Could the test be applied to a burdock seed head to see if it is stronger than the models?

## Summary

If the children have worked through all the seed challenges, not only will they have solved many practical problems but they will have sharpened their awareness of the natural world. Who can fail to wonder at the ingenuity that has gone into the various techniques for dispersing seeds, especially when one has tried to reproduce those techniques oneself? Children will have seen things they may never have noticed before even if these things have been on their doorsteps all the time. Finally, the observations will have been all the more vivid because they were made with a definite purpose in mind.

# 3 Time

## Introduction

Most teachers working through a project on time with their children would want to discuss the fundamental units of time such as 'the day' and 'the lunar month' as well as our arbitrary units of seconds and hours. Suggestions for such work are to be found in a number of publications, notably the Science 5/13 unit *Time* (published by Macdonald), and so are not dealt with here.

The work described here concerns itself not so much with the facts of time but with the design and construction of timing devices. Children will need to know how to use a stopwatch or stopclock measuring in seconds, or perhaps they could read a large wall clock with a sweeping second hand, though, of course, this is much harder. It would certainly be worth investing in a set of battery-operated digital stopwatches. These are relatively inexpensive and may have other functions such as a chronometer and beep alarm.

Most of our methods of measuring time fall into two broad categories. One kind of timer uses the slow movement of something or a slow process. This can be graduated so that smaller bits of time can be measured. A candle clock burns slowly down perhaps over a period of hours. If we mark its length into 'hour' sections then we have a 'slow moving' clock. A dripping water clock falls into this category as do a sand timer and the burning fuse on a stick of dynamite!

The second category consists of those devices which involve the counting of a lot of identical or similar movements. For instance, the swings of a pendulum or the vibrations of a quartz crystal. Indeed, a single rotation of our planet could be thought of as one of these identical movements. (What do we get if we count seven complete revolutions of the earth?)

On the other hand, if we view a single rotation of the earth as a 'slow moving' clock, then we may subdivide the day by observing the position of the sun or stars.

These approximate categories, then, are not exclusive but serve to start us thinking about timers and the way they work.

## UNIT 1
### Rolling marble

If your children have not used stopwatches before, they will need instructions and some preliminary practice before they begin this stage. Children enjoy timing themselves as they write out the alphabet or do ten press-ups but it is as well to include a few

tasks with which you can check their accuracy without having to be present when they do them. Use a traditional sand egg-timer that gives consistent results and ask them to time this. Alternatively, fix up a simple pendulum by hanging a 50 g mass from a length of string. Find out for yourself how many seconds it takes to swing ten times. As long as the length of the string is not altered, this time will remain the same for all those that use it. You will need to explain what you mean by one swing and also ask the children not to give it a push at the beginning.

Once the children have gained some proficiency in using their stopwatches they can try the following investigation which is in preparation for the challenge in Unit 2.

**1** Timing the rolling marble

### The challenge

Show the children how a desk (or a large board) can be tilted by placing cards under one end. Raise one end of the desk by about 5 cm. Now roll a marble (or a small ball) from one end to the other without pushing it at the start. The desk may need adjusting so that the marble rolls the length of the desk and not 'diagonally' to fall off the long edge (figure 2).

Give out stopwatches and ask the children to time the roll of your marble. Mention a few words about starting the stopwatch at the same time as the marble is released. 'Ready–steady–go' is useful. The marble on your table should take about 4 or 5 seconds, so now challenge the children in pairs to arrange their desks so that their marble takes, near enough, 10 seconds to roll off the desk.

*Without pushing your marble, make it roll from one edge to the other in as near 10 seconds as possible. Do this by changing only the slope of your desk.*

This challenge is designed for a flat-topped desk, about 120 cm long. If you have shorter desks, adapt the challenge to suit your conditions.

pile of cards

**2** The marble should roll the length of the desk

While the children are completing their task, they should be encouraged to test their slope three or four times to make sure they have got it right.

The condition of the desk surface will inevitably affect the consistency of the results, so you may have to be prepared to accept times of 1 second either side of the 10 seconds.

There are few technical problems in this challenge, so all children should achieve some degree of success, paving the way for the challenges that follow.

### Extension work

Those who finish their work quickly could be encouraged to make a 15 second timer — a much harder task because the marble may wander as it rolls, giving inconsistent results.

### Summary

You may decide at the end of the session to allow each pair to demonstrate their 10 second timer to the rest of the class. The children can reinforce their timing skills by timing each other. Could a team of six pairs time exactly 1 minute?

---

**SCIENCE PRINCIPLES TO HAVE IN MIND**
- **The effect of *gravity* on a falling body will be experienced.**
- **The *acceleration* of the marble as it descends the slope will be noticed by the children with the help of appropriate comments from the teacher.**
- **Your children may be able to appreciate that the higher the starting point of the marble, the more *potential energy* it will possess. How will this affect the time of descent?**

---

## UNIT 2
### Longest journey

The next challenge is closely related to the first but introduces a degree of open-endedness which was absent before. This makes it a practical problem which can be solved in a creative way because it incorporates that essential ingredient: design.

Ask the children how they would make the journey of the marble down the slope take even longer than 10 or 15 seconds. The answer you need to coax from them, amongst others, is to make its route longer by guiding it all over the table surface. Show them how they must guide their marble by sticking folded pieces of paper to the desk top using sticky tape (figure 3).

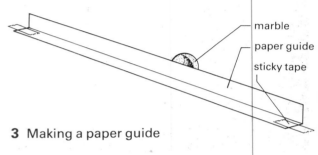

marble

paper guide

sticky tape

**3** Making a paper guide

**CHALLENGE 2**
*Find a way to make your marble take as long as possible to roll down your slope. You may use only the paper provided and 15 cm of sticky tape. The marble should touch the table top at all times and should not stop on the way.*

One way of extending the route of the marble is to make a zig-zag path down the desk but try to avoid suggesting this to the children as they may invent even better methods.

Prop up one end of the desk by about 2 or 3 cm. This gives a clear, positive roll to the marble. A set of identical books, or blocks of wood of equal thickness could be used in place of the cards used in the previous exercise. Dispense the sticky tape by sticking it lightly on to the desk surfaces and give out old pieces of sugar paper about 60 cm by 30 cm.

The children will find all kinds of subsidiary problems such as their marble rolling off the side of the desk or perhaps stopping before it has completed its journey. These are, of course, easily overcome without recourse to the teacher but you may find some unexpected difficulties arising where you did not expect them. A group of children who were tackling this problem recently had made a complicated, winding track for their marble to follow. Unfortunately, it consisted of a continuous

**4** A zig-zag guide system during its development

## Extension work

Set those who have achieved a satisfactory result and have time to spare the task of graduating their marble timer into 5 second sections with markers along the route (figure 5).

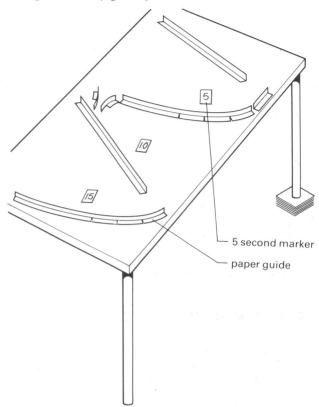

5 second marker

paper guide

**5** Marking 5 second intervals

guide, somewhat like a snake, resting on the desk top. The marble started well, above the paper guide, but on reaching the first bend its intended route took it beneath the guide! It simply rolled away and off the edge of the table. The children were rather surprised to see this happen and their teacher was even more surprised that they should have thought such an arrangement would work. The moral of the story is: (a) do not take your children's previous experience for granted and (b) some children need practical work to grasp even the seemingly obvious. Naturally, the teacher turned the situation into a useful discussion on how to correct the current problem and mentioned the effect of gravity on the marble as it rounded the bend.

Those children with plenty of experience in practical work might use their paper for purposes other than the guides you have shown them. I have seen 'flaps', 'curtains' and 'cattle grids' used to good effect. The guides, of course, need not be straight and it is probably worth pointing this out early on so that the children are aware of the wide variety of options open to them.

If you have made the challenge into a competition you will have to treat each group equally but if not, you may find some groups need more paper or sticky tape — so be prepared.

How could the children use their marble timer to measure 15 seconds or even one minute? (Use more than one marble.)

### SCIENCE PRINCIPLES TO HAVE IN MIND
- **The effect of gravity and the acceleration that this produces will be experienced by the children.**
- **The concept of friction will be met if the marble is slowed by rubbing on the paper guides.**
- **The bounciness of the guides may send the marble along interesting trajectories.**
- **All the time, the children are sharpening their awareness of the passage of time. By the end of the activity, most of them will know what 10 or 20 seconds 'feel' like.**

## UNIT 3 *(Part 1)*
### *Water-soak clock*

In Unit 3 we will challenge the children to design and make a timer using a particular principle. We will begin by explaining the task but before solving the problem we will guide the children through a series of investigations. This research will provide the children with some of the necessary experience upon which to base their ideas for solutions. The timer involves the principle that water soaks slowly into an absorbent material such as blotting paper.

Demonstrate this idea to the children, perhaps by hanging a paper towel in a jar of water and seeing how the water rises slowly upwards. Then set them the task of making a 2 minute timer using a substance that soaks up water in a similar way.

*Use the idea that some materials soak up water slowly to invent a 2 minute timer. It must be clear when your period of 2 minutes begins and ends.*

**6** Which will soak up water faster?

## Research

At this point explain the importance of research into the problem before making any design decisions. We are unlikely to find much of use in books, so our research will take the form of an investigation that we carry out ourselves.

When we make our timer what decisions must we make?

What will hold the water?

What material will best soak up the water? (The greatest 'length' of soak will probably be best.)
What shape will the material be: a circle, a strip, a rolled tube, a screwed up length?
What is the best position for the material: vertical, horizontal or at an angle? Could the water be made to soak downwards?
How will we mark the 2 minute level?

These questions should only serve to stimulate the children's interest in the challenge — we are not really in a position to answer them until we have researched the problem.

A worksheet like the one shown on page 37 will help the children to make some of the necessary decisions for the design of the timer. Of course, there are other ways of presenting this preliminary work. The worksheet serves only as an example. In fact, the research into the absorbency of materials could go on for a number of weeks but then there is the danger that the children will lose sight of the reason for doing it. One of the major gains in doing preliminary research is that children, when they have acquired certain knowledge, learn to apply it in a new situation. Make it clear, then, that you expect to see the ideas that come to light in their research being used in the construction of their timer.

Suitable materials to have available for the children might include blotting paper, paper towels, absorbent fabrics such as wool or cotton, toilet paper and string. Some children might suggest that a transparent tube filled with sand would work or perhaps some polythene folded into a 'capillary tube'.

Instead of marking the strips every centimetre, you could ask the children to fix the strips to a plastic ruler which, of course, already has a scale marked on it. Two small elastic bands slipped over the ruler will allow strips to be changed quickly and conveniently. The ruler will also make it easier to hold the strip upright in the jar. Alternatively, the strip could be marked and folded to hang on the rim of the jar, possibly fixed in place with a paper clip.

Once the children have finished their investigations, they will want to know what the others in the class have found out. They ought to find that a rolled strip soaks up more than a flat one of the same material and that a horizontal one does better than a vertical one. Be prepared for the results to show some inconsistencies, however, and encourage the children to have faith in their own findings. The true facts about the soakability of materials are not as important as the process through which the children are now working. As long as they have been as careful as they can in establishing their findings, then that is good enough for this exercise. Besides, if you try to reach a class consensus on the best arrangement for the 'soaker', the following design

## FINDING OUT ABOUT THE SOAKABILITY OF MATERIALS

1 Write down some materials that you think might be suitable for soaking up water.

_____   _____   _____

_____   _____   _____

2 Cut two equal size strips of different materials that you have mentioned above. Make a mark every centimetre from one end.

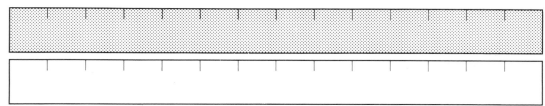

3 Pour water into two jam jars to a depth of 2 cm in each. Then have a race with your strips.

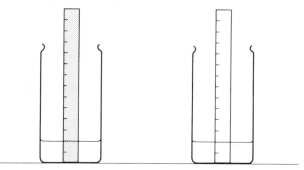

Which soaks up the most water in 2 minutes? Ask a friend to help you.

Which strip soaked up the most? _____

Check your result by doing it again.

4 Investigate these ideas in the same way.
Use equal strips of the same material each time.

a 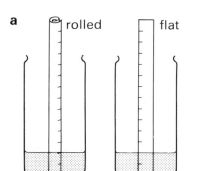 rolled  flat

b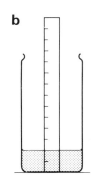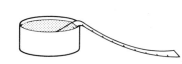

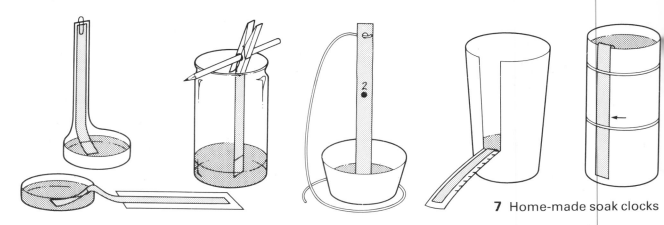

**7** Home-made soak clocks

and construction stage will produce rather similar results — something we would like to avoid.

## UNIT 3 (Part 2)
### Making the water-soak clock

Now that the children have spent time investigating the behaviour of absorbent materials, they should have a fairly clear idea of how to construct their 'timer'. Having the challenge in their minds will have made the research more meaningful. Now they can apply their pure science findings to a technical problem. They may, however, need reminding that this is what is expected of them. Children do not necessarily connect the events of two separate lessons, though they should be encouraged to do so.

If the previous research has been closely guided by the teacher, the children may now appreciate some time to investigate freely before they plan the construction of their device. For instance, some of them may have the idea that the water will soak downwards best and they may need the chance to try this out.

When they are ready, ask the children to draw their design for the timer. Make sure they understand what materials of construction they can use. Plastics, being waterproof, will be more suitable than card. A number of strips of absorbent material will be needed for each device — some for the preliminary trials and some for the final model. Elastic bands can be used to fix strips to supports or to mark water levels on containers. Staples and paper clips may be best for securing plastic components together. Shallow dishes can be cut from yogurt cartons, or perhaps you have petri dishes you can give the children. Felt tip pens may be useful for marking the 2 minute level on the absorbent material. These marks will 'explode' as the water reaches them. Check the children's designs for obvious impossibilities. Allow them to

make small mistakes that they can correct in a short time but persuade children to change their design if they are obviously going to have difficulties.

Figure 7 shows some possible solutions for the teacher to have in mind.

Your children will need to test and improve and test again until they are satisfied with their devices, so have plenty of absorbent material available.

### Extension work

When children have their timers functioning properly, ask them to graduate their devices. Can they mark half minute intervals for instance?

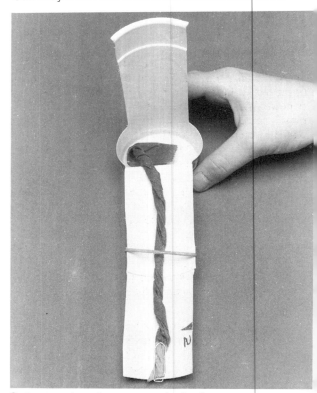

**8** A completed water-soak clock

## Summary

One way of summing up such a lesson would be to ask all the groups to start their timers at the same time and put their hands up when they think 2 minutes is up. If you are the only one using a stopwatch to measure the 2 minutes, you will find out who has been particularly successful.

Again, inconsistencies will mean that the times are only very approximate. Show by your attitude that this does not matter. What is important is that each group has tried its best to solve the problem in its own imaginative way.

> **SCIENCE PRINCIPLES TO HAVE IN MIND**
> **Water soaks through substances because of the attraction of its surface molecules to the molecules of these substances. This is sometimes called *capillary attraction*. The force is enough to overcome gravity up to a particular limit. If, however, the soaking material is horizontal, or even sloping downwards, then gravity does not have to be overcome and the water should soak further along.**

# UNIT 4
## *Pendulums*

While you tackled the work on the rolling marble and the water-soak clock, you may have discussed other examples of 'slow moving' clocks such as a candle clock or a sand timer. To add interest, you may have chosen to construct and demonstrate a water clock or a shadow clock.

Now we move on to a 'counting clock', in which a number of identical movements has to be accumulated to arrive at a particular time. A simple pendulum possesses this property but you might also mention the modern quartz watch which 'counts' vibrations of a crystal and possibly the electric clock which relies on a small electric motor to drive its hands round. (The many revolutions of the motor are 'counted' in this kind of clock.)

Make a simple pendulum by hanging a 10 g mass on a thread. Satisfy yourself that the following facts hold true:

a The time taken for the first ten swings is the same as that for the next ten swings. Each swing of the pendulum takes the same amount of time and this is why it can be used in a clock.
b Pendulums of different lengths take different times for one swing. Just watch two unequal-length pendulums swinging. They will be out of unison.
c If you add more mass to the pendulum bob, it makes no difference to the time of swing. Try the arrangement shown in figure 9. Release both pendulums simultaneously and they should swing together.
d Pendulums of the same length but swinging through different (small) arcs should take the same time for each swing (figure 10).

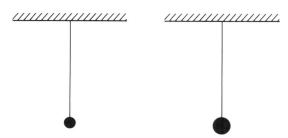

**9** Pendulums of equal length but different mass

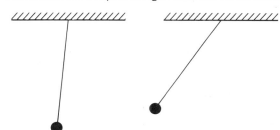

**10** Pendulums of equal length and mass

Once you have established these facts for yourself, see if the children can discover some of them.

### Preliminary investigations

The children will have to become familiar with the action of a variety of pendulums before they can understand the subtleties of the next challenge, and so the worksheet on page 40 has been designed to help them achieve this. Before you introduce the work, establish that, for our purposes, one swing of the pendulum means across and back again (figure 11).

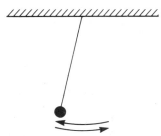

**11** One complete swing

# WORKSHEET TWO

## PENDULUMS

1  Make a pendulum.

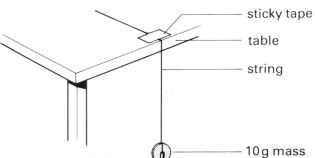

2  Complete this table for your pendulum.

Length of my pendulum is _____

| Number of swings | 10 | 20 | 30 | 40 | 50 |
|---|---|---|---|---|---|
| Time taken (seconds) | | | | | |

What do you notice about your results?

_____

Work out how long 100 swings would take. _____

3  Make two pendulums.

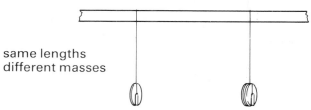

same lengths
different masses

Let them go at exactly the same time.

Do they swing almost together? _____

Try other masses to see if you get the same result.

4  Try this.

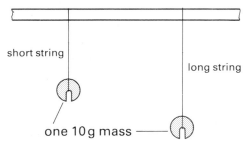

short string

long string

one 10 g mass ———

Which one swings faster? _____

Try different lengths.

Do you always get the same result? _____

The teacher will need to discuss the results of this work carefully with the children as the issues can easily become confused. The results of the activity in Sections 1 and 2, if they have been recorded with reasonable accuracy, should show that the time taken is proportional to the number of swings. Quite simply, then, it does not matter when you start timing the swinging pendulum — ten swings will always take about the same time. Children will notice that the values for the time taken form a sequence — 'they go up in equal steps'. They will need help in realising the implications of this.

In Section 3 the children should establish the fact that the mass of the pendulum bob is irrelevant to its period of swing. Again, they will need to discuss exactly what it is they have learnt.

**12** Timing ten swings of a pendulum

Section 4 must be understood if the children are to tackle the next problem. Perhaps this part of the investigation should be given more prominence or perhaps a second investigation should be devoted to it. The important thing that the children learn is that the longer a pendulum gets, the more slowly it swings. Equally true is the fact that the more slowly it swings, the more time it takes for a swing and this twist in the language often confuses children for a while. Get them to talk about their experiences and lead them to a clearer understanding with questions and answers.

Having carried out this scientific investigation for themselves, the children are now ready to try Challenge 4. This is not an open-ended problem because there is only one correct answer. It is a task, however, in which most children can come close enough to the answer required to feel that they have 'solved the problem'.

*Make a pendulum that swings back and forth in exactly 1 second. (Hint: Make your pendulum so that it swings back and forth ten times in 10 seconds.)*

The children should know by now that to alter the time of swing of a pendulum, they have to change the length. If they have not grasped this, perhaps they should be left to discover it now. There is a fixed length that will achieve the desired result so it might be a good idea to work this out for yourself before the children start to solve the problem.

### Extension work

Ask those who finish early to find the length of the pendulum that swings from left to right once in 1 second. This pendulum will, of course, be longer than the last one and will require a much higher point of support.

### Summary

It would be appropriate at the end of this lesson to see just how close each group has come to getting the correct pendulum length. If you record the lengths on the blackboard, you could use a calculator to work out the average result for the whole class. Have your correct pendulum set up ready to demonstrate for those who want to see.

The children could, of course, go on at this point to use their pendulums to time various activities such as the ones they encountered at the beginning of this topic.

---

**SCIENCE PRINCIPLES TO HAVE IN MIND**
- **The pendulum possesses different kinds of energy at different points in its swing. The energy of the raised bob is changed to 'movement' energy as it falls, which in turn changes back to the original 'raised' energy as the pendulum completes its swing.**
- **Can the children see when the pendulum is moving its fastest or when it is stationary for a fraction of a second? The pendulum is continuously accelerating and decelerating.**
- **Why does the pendulum eventually stop?**

---

A natural extension to this work on pendulums would be to investigate other devices that behave in a similar way. The children could be given a variety of likely materials and asked to make timers of their own design based on a to-and-fro movement (figure 13).

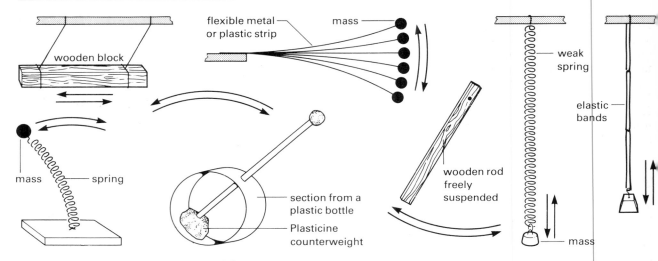

**13** More ways of getting a to-and-fro movement

## UNIT 5
### Twister alarm clock

This problem involves a large number of choices for the children both in making the timer and in inventing the alarm. The invention can be made with inexpensive 'recycled' materials and can be suspended beneath a desk or a chair. Figure 14 shows a twister.

There are many suitable variations on the length and mass of the components. A combination that works well is illustrated. If the threads are long and too close together, the twister will unwind too slowly and not jerk suddenly when it is completely unravelled. Shorter threads will result in a more prominent drop when the twister finishes. If the bar is heavy, it will start slowly but build up speed and jerk awkwardly at the end of its spin. A light bar will not have so much effect.

Show the children the principle involved in making a twister. Point out the violent jerk that can occur when it has completely unravelled, then define the problem to be solved.

*Make a twister alarm clock that makes an alarming noise exactly 4 minutes after it has been released. This would make it suitable for timing a hard boiled egg!*

This timer 'counts' a number of similar movements (each revolution of the bar) and indicates that the time is up by the sudden jerk that occurs when the thread finally unravels.

The children will need to consider the following points.

What will support their twister: string, cotton thread or wool? How long should it be?

What will the threads be fixed to? They can be taped to a desk top or tied more securely to the underside of a chair standing on a desk. A clamp stand could be used but this might limit the size of the device.

What will they use for a bar? A ruler, a block of wood, a card tube or even a bucket of sand?

How will they make it untwist in exactly 4 minutes? They will need to count the number of times they wind it up, and then release it and find out if this was enough or not. By trial and error they can quite quickly find the correct number of initial winds.

How will their alarm work? The more noise the better!

The children will need to try out more than one

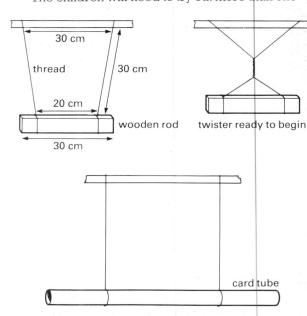

**14** A twister can be set up in a variety of ways

type of twister before they decide which is the most suitable for their design. It is probably best to organise the work in stages. First, make the 4 minute timer. Secondly, make the alarm. You might consider asking larger groups to work as a team, sharing out the tasks as efficiently as possible. A group of four, for instance, could be organised so that two construct the twister while the others work on the alarm system. Naturally, they would have to cooperate, otherwise the two parts might not be compatible.

## The alarm

The alarm must be triggered by the twister when it has unwound so many turns. This point is likely to be reached when the threads have unravelled completely but this does not have to be so. For instance, if something was hooked on to the threads so that it was released after perhaps 20 winds, then this would be satisfactory. Something falling from the twister can, of course, be made to make a noise. The alternative to something falling would be to have the bar hit something as it flicks round or as it drops to a certain level. Perhaps the sudden jerk can be made to shake some bell system attached to the rod. Finally, as the threads unwind, they pull apart. Could this movement trigger the alarm?

**15** Sounding the alarm

Have some noisy items such as tin plates, mugs and biscuit tins available. A pair of cymbals from the music department would work wonderfully, as would the bell from an old alarm clock.

Some possible solutions are illustrated in figure 16 and you might even consider using these as hints for those who are having difficulty. Many children will, undoubtedly, come up with their own original solutions and this is to be encouraged.

## Extension work

Ask those who need their imaginations stretching to graduate their device so that a sound is made every minute for the 4 minutes.

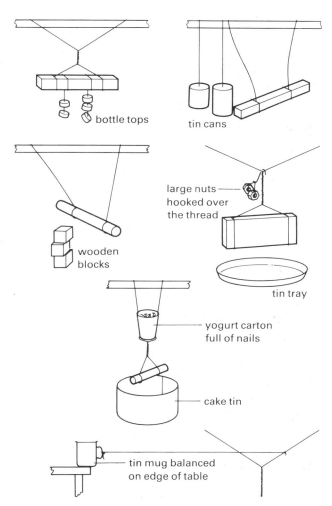

**16** A variety of alarms

## Summary

When each group has had the chance to develop its alarm clock, try getting all the groups to start their clocks at once. If you set a stopclock going for everyone to see, then as the 4 minutes draws to a close you should feel the mounting tension in the room. Whose alarm will go off prematurely and whose will be late? Full marks for those who get it right within 10 seconds.

If you have shown the children a wide variety of timing devices as they have worked through this topic, then you might feel it appropriate to conclude the work by asking them to make a timer of their choice that measures a time span also of their choice. The challenge would be to get their devices as accurate as they reasonably can. From water clocks and sand timers, to marbles falling through glue and the use of electric motors, there are plenty of designs to choose from.

# 4 Wheels

## Introduction

The work in this topic is not designed to teach children the scientific principles of wheels and axles but rather to encourage them to design and build various wheeled models that fulfil a particular function. They will be testing their models and improving them constantly by being scientific.

Probably the greatest problem in making wheeled models is attaching a wheel firmly to its axle. There is a number of suitable solutions to this problem but equally many methods result in failure and frustration both for the children and their teacher. In this topic, the wheels for most of the models are made from stiff card and so the children can design and cut out their own. Any stiff card will do as long as the children can cut it themselves and it does not bend too easily. For instance, thin corrugated card from a box, or off-cuts which may be obtained from a shop or factory will do.

In the later Units in this topic, a wooden axle made from commercially available dowel rod is required and a simple method for fixing this to the wheel is discussed.

## UNIT 1
### Inventing the wheel

We begin with a simple challenge for which the children will need free access to a wide variety of bits and pieces of junk.

*Draw and cut out from card a circle of radius 3 cm. Add anything you like to it to enable it to roll down a slope in a straight line without being pushed at the beginning.*

This is an easy introduction to the idea of solving a problem by making, testing and improving. If your children are not used to using a pair of compasses, they can simply draw round any suitably sized object such as the rim of a jam jar. You might expect your children to work alone on this problem as the equipment and materials are easily supplied. The children will still gain the benefit of discussing the problem with friends, but at the same time none of them will be able to sit back and let someone else do all the work.

The slope could be a desk or cupboard propped up with a brick or two and should not be too steep. The longer it is, however, the more challenging the problem will be. The 'anything' that the children add to their card disc will depend on what is available in the junk box and could, of course, include more card circles. Some may want to use their pencils or

something similar as axles, though this is not the only solution to the problem. Glue, paper clips and string should be available for those who want them. Plastic containers, bottle tops, corks and card may all be useful.

This problem is easily solved and enables all the children to experience some degree of success. Point out the importance of making sure that the problem is truly solved by expecting your children to try their wheels a number of times on the slope rather than depending on a single run.

If you have only one slope in the room, arrange a system whereby each child has, say, one go on the slope and then moves to the back of the queue. To avoid congestion at the slope, use more than one in the room or suggest that informal trials go on at each child's desk. The desk can be tilted with the help of a few blocks of wood, or it can be held up temporarily by a partner.

## Extension work

As with all the challenges in this book, it is wise to be prepared for the child who, by expertise or luck, solves the problem quickly. Also, some of the less able ones in the class will need more attention than others, so you will want to keep all the members of the class usefully occupied.

Challenge those who finish quickly to find as many different solutions to the problem as they can and be ready to explain to the rest of the class how they have done it. Alternatively, ask them to invent a method for making their wheel travel down the slope as slowly as possible.

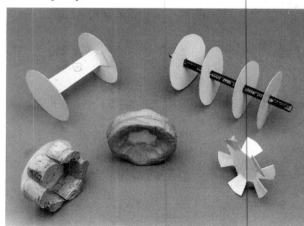

**1** Some solutions to Challenge 1

## Summary

When the children have finished, discuss with them the merits and drawbacks of each invention. Were the complicated ones the most successful or did simplicity rule the day? Ask the children to explain the problems they had in arriving at their final solutions. They may have noticed that those models with more than one wheel and the wheels widely separated go straighter than those with their wheels close together. Why should this be so?

Remind them that there are often many possible solutions to the simplest problem and that we should not always take the first one that comes into our head.

> **SCIENCE PRINCIPLES TO HAVE IN MIND**
> ● **What makes the wheel roll down the slope? Does it get faster as it nears the bottom? Gravity and the acceleration it produces play a part here.**
> ● **The children may have noticed that a single wheel in motion will stay upright because of its *inertia*. A stationary wheel, however, requires additional support. Compare this with a bicycle. Can it stand alone, riderless and without moving? How does a BMX rider keep his or her balance?**

**2** Will it work this time?

# UNIT 2
## Going round the bend

*Using any materials that you can find, make something that will turn a corner as it rolls down a slope.*

The children will need to have ready access to a slope and curved course for their wheel arrangement to follow (figure 2). You might fix up one slope that all the class uses but perhaps a more convenient way is to use the children's desks propped up on equal sized blocks of wood. If the slope is covered with paper, the curve can be marked clearly on it. Alternatively, a Plasticine 'fence' or a series of small sticky labels could define the route the wheel must take. A quick and convenient way to mark the route would be to use a piece of chalk tied to a length of string and, using the corner of the desk as the centre, draw a quarter circle on the desk. Whichever method you use, remember that the curve should be part of a circle or the children will find it impossible to solve the problem.

There are two ways in which the children might try to solve this problem. The first is to make one end

of the wheel system smaller than the other (figure 3a) and the second is to devise a steering mechanism (figure 3b).

You need not explain these ideas to the children and do not be disappointed if none of them even

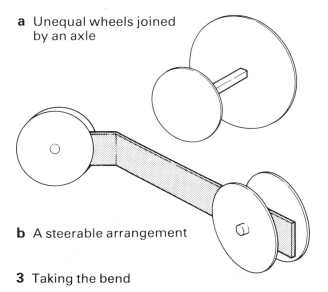

**a** Unequal wheels joined by an axle

**b** A steerable arrangement

**3** Taking the bend

considers the ideas you have in mind. They should do the thinking, perhaps make mistakes and then be encouraged to correct them. Some of their solutions may be surprisingly simple and quickly achieved. Would, for example, a plastic carton such as a yogurt pot with the right dimensions fulfil the brief? If a bright (or lucky) child completes his or her task in a short time, be ready to change the rules. Draw a different shaped curve to be followed and the problems will begin all over again.

The children will have to overcome the problem of fixing things together and a few words of advice may be useful before construction begins. It seems to take children a long time to realise that surfaces that are to be glued together should have large surface areas. You cannot glue a card wheel on to the end of a pencil-thin rod and expect it to hold unless you have exceptionally strong, fast-setting glue. Gluing plastics also poses a problem because the correct glue must be used. There are times when staples or paper clips are more effective. Sometimes pieces can be slotted together with no need for glue.

Finally, too much glue on a surface means a long wait for it to dry to its full strength. An effective and less wasteful alternative is to spread a thin layer of glue on the surface in question and then to rub it gently with a finger until it becomes tacky. If the two surfaces are now held together tightly for a count of 100, the joint should have immediate strength.

The emphasis in solving this problem will be on trial and error, although a lot of scientific observation and hypothesising will go on at the same time.

> Did the wheel turn too tight a curve?
> Perhaps if the axle is lengthened the turn will improve.

Encourage the children to be accurate and test their model more than once on the slope. The first test run, after all, may have been a freak and not typical.

## Extension work

You could challenge an able group of children to make a wheel that can be adjusted to roll along a variety of curves. This might be achieved by having a variable-length axle with unequal wheels, or a steering device as mentioned before.

## Summary

If time permits, you could allow groups of children to 'visit' others at their desks for a demonstration of their model. In a class discussion you might consider which wheels are best and why. What can be learnt from those that do not work so well? What further improvements would the children make if they had more time?

## UNIT 3 (Part 1)
### The buggy

The remaining challenges in the Wheels topic depend on the construction of a simple wheeled vehicle which can be made by the children in the classroom or laboratory. In Part 1 we make the buggy; and in Part 2 we set the children a challenge using it.

To overcome the problem of fixing the axles to the wheels, some preparation may be required by the teacher. A number of solutions to the problem are illustrated in figure 4. The axle in each case is a length of 6 mm (¼ inch) dowel rod which is easily obtained from any DIY shop. It is inexpensive and can be sawn or snapped into suitable lengths of about 6 cm.

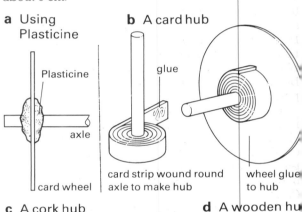

**a** Using Plasticine — Plasticine, axle, card wheel

**b** A card hub — glue, card strip wound round axle to make hub, wheel glued to hub

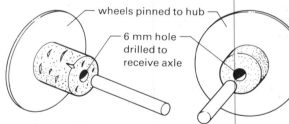

**c** A cork hub — wheels pinned to hub, 6 mm hole drilled to receive axle

**d** A wooden hub

**4** Four ways of fixing a wheel to an axle

All methods have the great advantage that the children can make card wheels to their own design and swap them around as they try out different combinations.

The card hub requires little preparation by the teacher because the children can make it themselves. It can be a time consuming and messy job in the hands of the inexperienced, however, and is not as strong as some of the other methods. Equally the Plasticine needs little teacher preparation but is rather a flimsy answer to the problem. The method of using wooden blocks works well and once the components are made they can be used year after year. The blocks can be made out of a 3 or 4 cm diameter, smooth branch of a tree. Cut the branch into 10 cm sections, drill a 6 mm hole into each end and then cut into slices about 2 cm thick (figure 5).

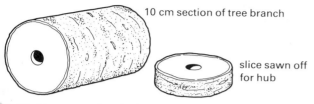

10 cm section of tree branch

slice sawn off for hub

**5** Making wooden hubs

In fact, any piece of softwood will do — it does not have to be a branch or even cylindrical but do arrange things so that the drawing pins that fix the wheel to the block are stuck into the end grain of the wood so that they can be easily removed. The hole through the wood does not have to be central but should be as near perpendicular to the face of the block as possible. When the wheel is pinned to the block, care should be taken to centre the hole in the block over the middle of the wheel so that even if the block is off centre the axle will be correctly positioned.

Because the card wheels need to be interchangeable for some of the following challenges, some difficulty may be encountered in continually removing and replacing the drawing pins. To overcome this problem in later Units, the method shown could be employed by the children (figure 6).

Whichever method you use, try it out first and satisfy yourself that your particular children can cope with the task of assembly without too much help from you.

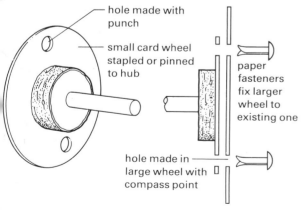

hole made with punch

small card wheel stapled or pinned to hub

paper fasteners fix larger wheel to existing one

hole made in large wheel with compass point

**6** Using paper fasteners to secure a larger wheel

## Finding the centre of the wheel

If compasses are used to draw the wheels on card, then there is no problem about finding the centre of the wheel. If, however, the children draw around

circular objects, they will need a method for finding the centres of their discs. This might be a chance to introduce a preliminary, problem solving, maths lesson. Give the children a circle of paper and ask them to devise as many ways as possible for finding the centre of the circle. How may ways can you think of? (See figure 7).

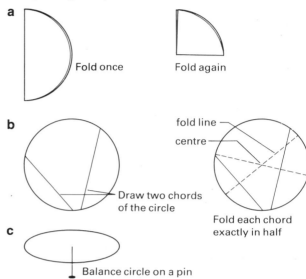

**a**

Fold once

Fold again

**b**

Draw two chords of the circle

fold line

centre

Fold each chord exactly in half

**c**

Balance circle on a pin

**7** Finding the centre of a circle

To find the centre of a card wheel, simply draw round the wheel on to a scrap piece of paper, find the centre of the paper circle and, placing this exactly on top of the card wheel, prick a small hole through the centre with a pin or pencil point.

## Making the buggy

The children could make their buggy by following a simple worksheet such as the one on page 48.

The wheel sizes are not critical though, of course, they should be larger than the wood blocks. The bulldog clips will need to have holes in their handles

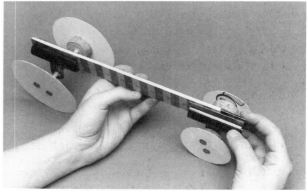

**8** Completing the buggy

# WORKSHEET ONE

## HOW TO MAKE A BUGGY

You will need:

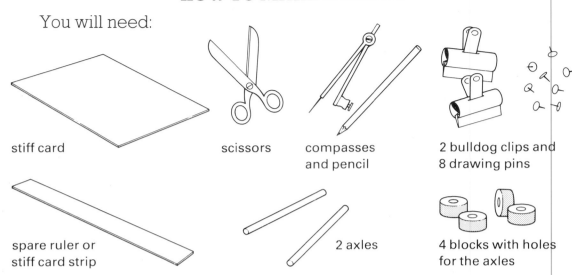

stiff card　　　　　scissors　　　compasses　　　2 bulldog clips and
　　　　　　　　　　　　　　　　　and pencil　　　8 drawing pins

spare ruler or　　　　　　　　　　　　2 axles　　　4 blocks with holes
stiff card strip　　　　　　　　　　　　　　　　　for the axles

1 Draw two wheels on the card 3 cm in radius.
2 Draw two wheels 5 cm in radius.
3 Cut out the four wheels.
4 Mark the centre of each wheel.
5 Make sure the hole in the block is over the centre of the
　wheel. Then fix the wheel to the block with drawing pins.
6 Fix both bulldog clips to the ruler.

This is the buggy chassis

7 Now complete
　the buggy.

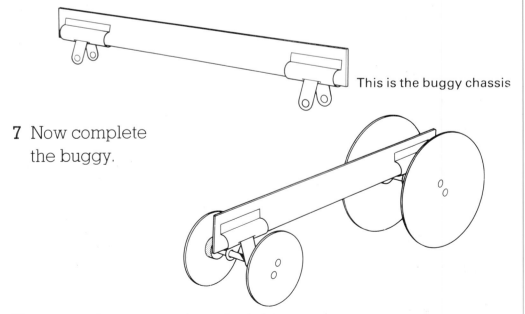

Does your buggy run in a straight
line? Try it down a slope.

large enough to take the dowel rod axles. The buggies can be dismantled at the end of the lesson for storage or the components can even be shared with other classes, the children simply keeping their own wheels until they are required again.

## Extension work

When the children have finished their buggy, they will need to see that it runs properly in a straight line. This could be done on a slope set up for the purpose or simply across the floor of the room. They can experiment with the length of the wheel base by changing the position of the bulldog clips. What difference does this make? Can the children find alternative ways of fixing the clips to the ruler? Will they clip on top of the ruler, for instance, instead of underneath?

Ask those with time to spare to design a steering device for their buggy and to try it out. This might be achieved by employing a card chassis which can be 'bent' round corners. Alternatively, is it possible to make the front bulldog clip swivel by clipping it to a vertical rod which in turn is fixed to the ruler?

## UNIT 3 (Part 2)
### Bumpers

Now that the children have a wheeled vehicle we can set them a variety of problems. The first is to design a safety bumper for their buggy.

When a vehicle crashes into something there are a number of safety features that can help to absorb the impact. One of these is a construction at the front of the vehicle which either crumples on impact or compresses temporarily like the thick rubber surround on fair-ground bumper cars. We could ask the children to make a bumper for their buggy that does one of these two things.

Before presenting the children with this challenge, show them how to make a simple seat for the buggy and put a 'driver' in it. This seat can be conveniently made out of a compartment from a cardboard egg carton or a piece cut from a toilet roll

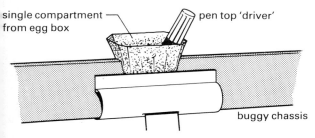

**9** Fixing a driving seat on the chassis

tube. The driver could be a plastic pen top or something similar. It must, of course, sit loosely in the same position in the seat each time (figure 9).

The next thing to do is to devise a situation in which the buggy can crash. Tilt a desk against a wall and let the buggy roll down with the driver on board. If the driver is thrown out when the buggy hits the wall, we could have a severe injury on our hands. Set the children the task of preventing the driver from falling out and needing hospital treatment.

*Design and make a safety bumper which can be clipped on to the front of your buggy. The bumper should prevent the driver from being thrown out of the seat in a crash.*

If the speed at which the buggy rolls down is too great, then nothing will prevent the driver from being thrown out. To overcome this problem (a) do not make the slope too great and (b) ask the children to find a position on the slope from which their buggy can be released so that the driver is only just thrown out. Under these conditions, the addition of a wide variety of bumpers should have the desired effect.

It is possible in this challenge that the children may lack a variety of ideas so the preliminary discussion with the class should provide plenty of starting points.

Ask the children to suggest ideas for the construction of their bumpers.

Which materials will be most effective?
Which materials will crumple and which will give a springy resistance?
Should you use a combination of both kinds of bumper — crumply and springy?

If you make a crumple-type bumper, be prepared to make a number of identical ones as each one will be destroyed in the test.

## Research

The following ideas could be carried out with the class looking on and making observations and suggestions for further investigations. Alternatively, and perhaps more effectively, the children could be asked to make the investigations for themselves.

Drop a suitable wooden block on to a variety of materials such as foam rubber, Plasticine, pieces of expanded polystyrene or a partially inflated balloon. Which deaden the fall most effectively? How can we measure how much the fall has been deadened? Does the thickness of the material matter? How much of a dent is there each time?

Do the same on various pieces of paper that have been folded in such a way that their shape is destroyed when the block lands. For instance, the paper could be rolled into a cylinder and stood on end or it could be folded into an arch before the block is dropped. Again, which kind of construction absorbs the impact well? Fold other materials such as cooking foil or card.

The children will need time to discover that simply adding a small piece of foam to the front of the buggy is probably insufficient to cushion the impact. If possible give them half an hour in which to do some more informal research using their buggy and various materials before asking them to produce a design drawing for their bumper. In any event, persuade the children to try as wide a variety of materials and methods as possible before they settle for the design which seems the best.

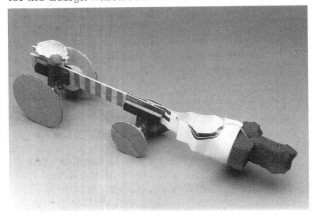

**10** This bumper is made from a folded plastic carton and a shaped piece of foam

## Extension work

If the problem is solved too easily by the children or they are keen enough to extend their investigation, ask them to increase the speed of impact and design a more substantial bumper.

An interesting and more challenging variation on the bumper theme would be to limit the children's choice of construction materials to, say, one sheet of A4 paper and some glue. Or could you limit them to a strip of plastic cut from a lemonade bottle? The paper bumper would require a 'crumple' design, while the plastic would probably employ the 'springy' principle.

This idea has interesting connections with the egg box challenge in Chapter 5 and it might be interesting to link the two.

## Summary

Do the children know of other safety features on vehicles? How important do they think these are? Could they invent a seatbelt test using their buggy?

**SCIENCE PRINCIPLES TO HAVE IN MIND**
● **How are shocks absorbed in the suspension of a car or in the wheels of a bicycle? Something springy is employed.**
● **How do we cushion ourselves if we see that we are going to run into an obstacle? We put an arm out that subsequently 'collapses' to absorb the crash.**
● **What happens if we try to hammer a nail into a piece of wood resting on a soft surface? The impact of the hammer is absorbed by the soft surface and the task becomes extremely difficult.**
● **How are breakable goods packed to prevent damage? Corrugated card and squashy packing material are designed to absorb impact.**

## UNIT 4
## *Elastic band motor*

The children will become excited at the prospect of fitting a 'motor' to their buggy especially if they are going to be fully involved in discovering the most efficient arrangement.

Show them one way of driving an axle using an elastic band (figure 11). If you demonstrate with an uncut elastic band, then the children can choose later whether to leave it double or have a single strand. This is often a good ploy in presenting problems for children to solve — demonstrate an inefficient arrangement so that the children can easily improve on it!

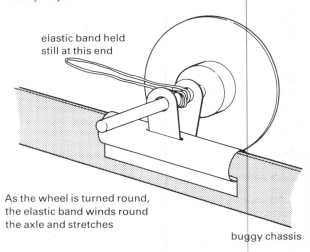

elastic band held
still at this end

As the wheel is turned round,
the elastic band winds round
the axle and stretches

buggy chassis

**11** An elastic band motor

Avoid suggesting any particular arrangement for the motor on the buggy. With this in mind, hold the free end of the band in your hand and simply let the children see how the single wheel turns. They can translate what they see into a working motor later by trial and error. You might suggest to them at this stage that the band does not have to be attached directly to the axle; it could be connected by a length of thread. The thread wraps itself around the axle as it is wound up.

*Attach one 'standard' elastic band to your buggy so that it drives the buggy as far as possible across the room. Besides fixing the 'motor' you will need to change the size of the drive wheels so that the maximum distance is achieved.*

## Fixing the elastic band

One end of the band (or thread) needs to be fixed to the axle holding the drive wheels. It is not sufficient to simply tie it around the axle as this will invariably result in slipping. You could let the children work on this problem themselves or give them some hints. A drawing pin driven into the centre of the axle will anchor the band but the children will be unable to remove the axle from the bulldog clip with this in position. A more satisfactory solution is to fix a staple close to the axle so that the band can be fixed to this and the axle can still be slid out of the bulldog clip holes (figure 12). This simple task could be done by the teacher before the lesson to save time.

**12** A staple fixed to the axle for anchoring the elastic band

The other end of the elastic band can easily be fixed to the leading bulldog clip or in a number of alternative positions. The children might need to experiment with the position of this anchor point to achieve maximum effect. Should the band, for instance, be slack or in tension before it is wound up?

## The size of the drive wheels

If the buggy is to travel as far as possible, the children will have to fit fairly large drive wheels (about 15 cm in diameter). If, however, the wheels are too large, the elastic band will be unable to drive the wheels at all. Once again we encounter the important technological concept of optimum

conditions for the best performance. Your children may need the idea of 'large wheel circumference equals greater distance' suggested to them if they have not experienced this before.

The children may suffer other minor problems in getting their vehicle to travel as far as possible. The wheels will have to be well cut and properly aligned for a straight run, the elastic band may get snarled up in the bulldog clips, and friction between the axle and the chassis might prevent a smooth run. This, however, is the stuff of problem solving and should be easily managed by the children as long as they are encouraged to be analytical and to persevere until they have a satisfactory result.

In a mixed ability class, of course, what is satisfactory for one child will be otherwise for another. The teacher will decide if a child has done his or her best and whether to expect a greater effort. Such is the nature of open-ended work that we should expect the response that we know is appropriate from each child.

## Extension work

It is unlikely that children will need to be extended after such a challenge because they can always improve their current model to increase its range. If, however, there are some keen to take their work further, ask them to fit a steering device to their buggy so that it can drive around in circles.

Alternatively, some children might like to look into the question of speed, and design a racing buggy. They will probably already know that smaller wheels, friction and elastic band size will influence the buggy's performance.

**SCIENCE PRINCIPLES TO HAVE IN MIND**
● **Where does the energy come from to drive the buggy? What are the energy changes from winding up the wheels to when the buggy comes to rest?**
● **The principle involving the force required by the elastic band to turn the wheels is a difficult one but some children may be able to understand that a thicker axle would allow a weaker force to start the wheel turning. Another way of putting this is to say that a thicker axle will promote a greater initial acceleration for a given elastic force. Even if children cannot understand or explain this in words, they can experience this principle of moments when they wind up a small and then a large wheel on their buggy. It should be easier to turn the larger wheel if it is held at its edge.**

## UNIT 5
### *Wobbly wheels*

This final design brief involving the buggy will draw from the children their skills in both science and craft. The scientific aspect is concerned with the effect of eccentric wheels. How can we harness the action of wobbly wheels to produce the desired effect? The artistic part of the project involves the making of the toy that is to wobble.

Almost certainly the best way for the children to experiment with various wheel combinations is for them to be able to change their wheels quickly and easily by using the paper fastener system described in figure 6 of this chapter. Have plenty of card ready so that they can try different wheel shapes and sizes.

*Using the chassis of your buggy, design and make a toy that either bobs up and down or wobbles from side to side.*

**13** An investigation into 'wobbles'

## Research

You could allow the children to experiment and find out for themselves how to make their buggy have an up-and-down movement, a rocking movement or a side-to-side movement. Ask them to make the movement as pronounced as possible and perhaps make a record of their findings.

For those who need more guidance through this research phase, a worksheet such as the one on page 53 might help.

The children will realise that when four oval wheels are used, the starting position of these as the buggy is pulled along will influence the type of movement. They can all run 'parallel' to each other

by starting at similar points on their circumferences (figure 14a) or, alternatively, they can be made to run out of unison. The 'parallel' movement will produce a level up-and-down action, while the alternative is a see-saw movement of the chassis (figure 14b).

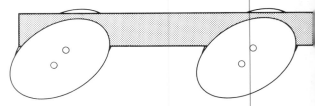

**14a** Wheels moving parallel to each other produce a level up-and-down motion

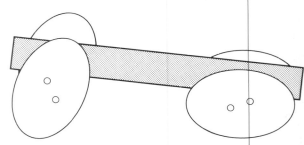

**14b** If the front and back wheels are started out of phase, a see-saw movement will result

The oval wheels, if arranged out of parallel on one axle, can be made to produce a wobble from side to side (figure 15).

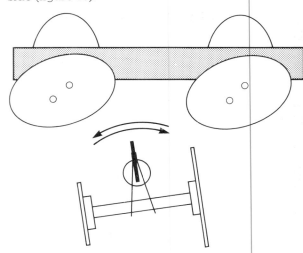

**15** A side-to-side wobble

The movements described above can be achieved by using circular wheels fixed off-centre at the axles. This should be discovered by the children in the second part of the worksheet.

# WORKSHEET TWO

## WOBBLY WHEELS

Your buggy can be made to wobble in different ways.

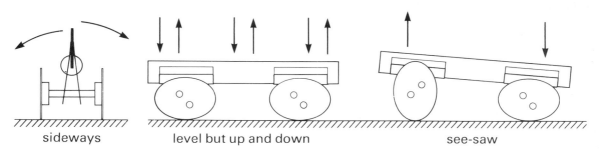

sideways      level but up and down      see-saw

1   Make some wheels
like this.

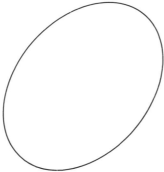

Fix them to your buggy
at their centre
and try them.

What movement do you get?
Sideways ___ Up and down ___ See-saw ___ (tick)
Can you make other movements with your oval wheels? Tick
these too.

2   Fix your circular wheels like this:

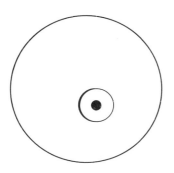 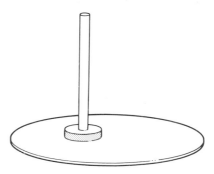

What movements can you get?

3   Make some other funny shaped wheels and fix them to your
buggy.
Draw the wheels and describe the movements you get.

Finally, the children may find some even more strange movements as they experiment with other unusual wheel shapes and combinations. All the better if they can discover their own.

When the children have discovered what is possible in the way of eccentric movements, discuss with them the sort of toys one would expect to bob up and down or wobble. They might suggest a duck, a snake, a boat at sea, a kangaroo and many others. Their model has to clip into the bulldog clips on the buggy chassis so it must be designed with this in mind. It could simply be a cardboard cut-out or, if time permits, they could tackle the job in three dimensions. The wheels, of course, can be suitably decorated as well as the body of the toy. The completed model can be pulled along by a piece of string — or perhaps the elastic motors are still in position!

## Planning on paper

The children will need to plan what they are going to do rather than rush in with the first idea that comes into their heads. Begin with doodles showing a number of ideas for the toy shape or wheel arrangements. Next a design drawing, or series of drawings, can be made. These drawings should be clearly labelled and perhaps show various views of the final model. When the children get to the construction stage, they should know exactly what they want to do as a result of such thorough preparation. All the same, they will want to make changes to their original design as they proceed and more ideas come to light.

## Extension work

If children have time, they may be able to make a foreground to their toy to give it greater effect. This is especially appropriate if they have made something like a boat or an animal.

Very keen and able pupils could be challenged to fix something to one of the wheels that in turn operates something on the toy.

**SCIENCE PRINCIPLES TO HAVE IN MIND**
Eccentric wheels are used to drive components in many machines such as sewing machines. The children may not have seen the internal workings of such machines but this fact is worth pointing out to them. Ask the children to imagine their buggies held still on a moving conveyor belt. An up-and-down movement will be produced which is similar to the movements required in some machines.

# 5 Paper Structures

## Introduction

The framework supporting a body is sometimes visible and sometimes not. The structure of a steel electricity pylon is clearly visible, while our bodies are supported by an unseen framework of bones. A suspension bridge displays its graceful form very obviously but what do we know about the underlying structure of an upholstered settee or a concrete skyscraper?

Supportive structures need to be strong but not cumbersome. Those on show need to be aesthetically pleasing though this often happens without conscious effort when they are designed for maximum efficiency.

The following challenges, while primarily designed to give children confidence in solving practical problems, set out to explore basic principles in creating strong and efficient structures. These principles will hold true whether the structures are made of steel, concrete or paper.

It is important in this topic that children are shown numerous examples of the structures around us. They should see not only the obvious ones in bridges, buildings and towers, but those nearer to home such as the human skeleton, furniture both in school and at home, fencing, playground equipment, bicycle frames and many other examples. The points to look for are the *materials* that are used in the construction and the *shapes* that give the structure its strength. Look at tubular steel furniture and find a similarity with the tubular shape of a chicken bone sawn in half. How is the stem of a large, tall plant such as hogweed built for strength? Look at the angular structure of metal shelving. How do folds give the necessary strength? Why do we not make bicycle frames from solid metal bars?

## UNIT 1
### Paper tower

To start children thinking about structures, we can give them a problem which is easily solved and yet has potential for close observation and analysis. The faster workers in the class should be encouraged to take their investigation as far as possible.

*Using only a sheet of A4 paper, make a 'tower' that can support a 1 kg mass 21 cm above the floor surface. There are many ways this can be done, so discover and record as many as you can.*

The width of the A4 paper is exactly 21 cm.

The floor is probably the safest place to do this work as the kilogram mass will fall off the trial structures a number of times. Give the children a piece of card to place their tower on and another piece to hold the mass on top of the tower. This card should not be attached to the tower. This is all they should need. No sticky tape, no glue. Part of the problem will be to fix together the free edges of the paper if the children feel this is necessary.

The children can record their successes as plan drawings like the ones in figure 1.

**1** A way to record successful paper towers

Impress upon the children that you are looking for the *strongest* tower, so even if they have found a number of arrangements that hold a kilogram they should continue their investigation to find the strongest.

They should be encouraged to lower the kilogram mass slowly on to the tower, watch what happens and analyse what is wrong with a tower that collapses. They may notice, for instance, that the walls buckle at a particular point. If this is so, they must remedy the defect, perhaps with an extra fold in the right place. Analysing what is wrong with a

**2** Loading a paper tower

'solution' to a problem is an essential part of the problem solving process and is a point at which many children give up easily if they are not encouraged. Initial failure is not a reason for giving up.

## Extension work

There are many variations on this idea, so if some of your children need more to do, set them the problem of building a tower with A4 paper which is only 10 cm high but which holds as great a mass as possible. They might choose to cut their paper in order to achieve this.

## Summary

Paper bends easily, so the force that supports the kilogram mass must act 'through' the paper. The children will have found that if the paper starts to buckle, the force due to the mass simply continues this buckling process until the tower collapses. Folds and curves help to prevent the initial buckle. If, in the discussion at the end of the lesson, the children have appreciated these points, then they will have done well.

> **SCIENCE PRINCIPLES TO HAVE IN MIND**
> **Materials that are seemingly flimsy can be strengthened by folding them in various ways. This makes possible the use of construction materials that are relatively light and inexpensive.**

## UNIT 2
### Egg box

The domed shape of an egg is a structure that the children may not have considered before. An egg shell is certainly built cost-effectively. There is no wasted material here and yet there is enough strength to protect the contents in the crowded surroundings of the nest. Can the children suggest other examples of this type of structure such as domed roofs or a motorcycle crash helmet? The egg box itself is often built to this shape though this is primarily to hold the egg securely in place. A secondary function of the shape of the box is, however, to provide enough strength to prevent the egg from being crushed in a shopping bag or on supermarket shelves.

It is the problem of holding and protecting eggs to which we now turn the children's attention. Before they try to solve the problem, there is some research that can be done to help them in their decision making.

 **CHALLENGE 2**

*Design and make a container to hold a single egg using only one A4 sheet of card. The container should protect the egg against pressure or impact from all sides. For example, imagine the egg being carried in a full shopping bag or being dropped accidentally on to a table surface.*

## Research

In constructing their 'egg box' the children will need to prevent the card container from bending or buckling in various places. How this might be done is suggested in the worksheet on page 57.

The children should now realise that a strip of cardboard (or even steel) is weak when bent in a direction perpendicular to its surface, but resistant to bending in a direction in its own plane. If two strips of card are fixed at right-angles to each other along their length, the resulting strut has strength in all directions. Can they now apply their findings to the practical problem at hand?

First you need some eggs — not real ones but perhaps wooden or marble ornamental eggs. Or perhaps you could use some real (empty) shells that have been taped back together? In the absence of any of these, you could use some screwed up tissue paper that has been taped together into approximately the right shape. If you want to alter the challenge slightly, you could design individual boxes for tomatoes, pears or bananas.

Children will have seen chocolate Easter egg boxes and this will give them a clue to one answer to the problem. For those who are stuck and cannot even get started, suggest that they begin by making a cylinder to surround the egg. They can then think about a top and a base and then about how to stop the cylinder from being squeezed from the side. One would expect to see strengthening 'fins' and 'angles' glued on the outside or inside of the container. Impress upon the children that they should try to apply the lessons learnt in the previous exercise to the construction of their box — some children will not do this automatically. The box, of course, will need to stand up and must not roll off the table so allowances must be made for this. The children will have a wider choice of solutions if you make it clear that the box need not completely cover the egg. For instance, a cage-like structure with the egg visible through the protective 'bars' is perfectly all right.

If children are thrown too quickly into this challenge, the results may be disappointing because they will not have a variety of ideas. The research time will be useful but so, too, will the preliminary discussions.

# WORKSHEET

## EXTRA STRENGTH

How can we strengthen a strip of card so that it does not bend?
Try these activities and find out.

1  Cut four equal strips of card like this.

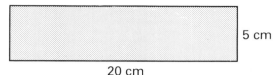

5 cm

20 cm

2  Mark the centre of each strip.

3  Place one strip across two desks like this and loop a thread
   around its centre.

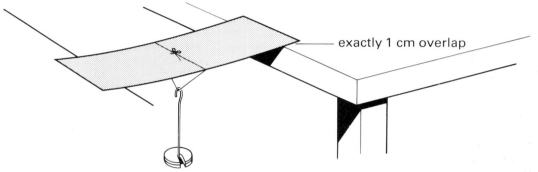

exactly 1 cm overlap

4  Load the strip, 10 grams at a time, until it falls. Provide some
   form of soft landing for your masses.

5  Record your results in a table like this:

| Shape of strip from the end | Mass that makes it collapse (grams) | Where does strip give way? |
|---|---|---|
|  |  |  |

Copy the table on to another sheet of paper.

6  Fold these strips and load them in the same way. Record your
   results in the table.

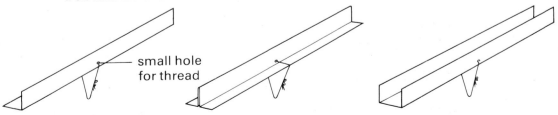

small hole
for thread

7  Explain how you can make a card strip stronger without using
   any extra card. Try to explain why it works.

8  If you have time, try some folds of your own.

**3** A variety of reinforced egg boxes

If you think it necessary, ask your children to make some initial sketches of a variety of possible solutions. If they find it difficult to draw their three-dimensional ideas, get them to make plan and side views of their model. In the end, the teacher must decide the best time to let his or her children proceed to construction.

## Testing

The boxes can be tested in a variety of ways — by loading with masses or by repeatedly dropping them until they break. Probably the best test under the circumstances is a subjective one. The children can feel how strong their boxes are by gently squeezing them. They can compare them with a real egg box. If they are stronger, then they have done well — though, of course, more card will have been used in the construction of their models.

## Extension work

If the children make a successful box, they can be encouraged to decorate it ready for commercial production.

## Summary

How much variety is there in the solutions to this problem? Is there really only one correct way to build an egg box?

Have the current manufacturers got it right or can the children suggest improvements to the egg boxes on the market today? Consider different materials and shapes, and ways of fixing the compartments together.

---

**SCIENCE PRINCIPLES TO HAVE IN MIND**
- **The force needed to bend a rod depends, amongst other things, on its thickness.**
- **A flat strip is 'thick' in one direction but not in another. Two strips at right angles to each other make a light, strong combination that prevents bending. See examples of steel girders and metal furniture.**

---

# UNIT 3
## Cantilever

A cantilever is a structure that sticks out from a support. It usually has to bear a load of some kind. Examples are the crane and its load, and the shop sign that hangs out over the street. It is most likely to break off at the point of support and so it is usually built more strongly there. Think of an angler landing a huge fish. His rod is most likely to break where he is holding it, so it is thicker at this point. The Forth rail bridge is a cantilever bridge. Each section is built like two arms reaching out to touch each other. The structure is clearly strongest at the point of support. There are further examples of the cantilever in the bone structure of large animals such as *Tyrannosaurus rex* and even *Homo sapiens*.

The following challenge involves the principle of the cantilever together with the important structural fact that the triangle, as opposed to any other polygon, is a rigid shape even when the sides are loosely jointed. However, the children need not be aware of either of these principles in order to tackle the problem. They can learn by discovery.

You will need to supply each group of children with a strong card bracket stapled to the wall and a quantity of card strips with a hole punched in each end (figure 4). These will be fixed together with brass paper fasteners.

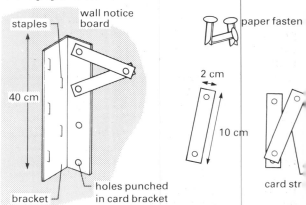

**4** The card wall bracket with strips and fasteners

Keep the strips about the length shown in the illustration or perhaps shorter. If you use longer ones, the whole structure will become ungainly and twist out of shape.

 *Using only the card strips and the paper fasteners, construct a cantilever out from your bracket as far as you can go.*

The classroom will have to be arranged appropriately for this lesson. Fix the brackets to notice boards and give the children as much room as possible at the walls.

The joints will all be loose, so the children cannot help but discover that they must use a triangular structure in order to build outwards. They may find that they require strips longer than the ones they are given in order to complete a particular arrangement. You could allow them a limited number of these or simply tell them they cannot have them. They could, of course, be allowed to make shorter strips by cutting and punching their own holes, so have some hole punches ready.

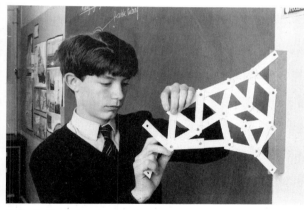

**5** Building the cantilever with card strips

Eventually they will find that as their cantilever gets longer it starts to twist over. An answer to this problem might be to build a second supportive cantilever by the side of the first but it is probably best to ask the children to support their structure by simply holding it loosely out from the wall (though not by supporting its weight).

You might provide an extra challenge by asking the children to use as few card strips as possible in their construction, or by giving them a fixed number, say 30, and asking them to build as far as possible with these.

Some children will decide to use double or even treble struts for added strength. Will you disallow this from the beginning or will you leave it to the children to 'invent' this idea?

## Summary

If you introduce the added stimulus of a time limit on construction, then at the end you could discuss why some groups were able to work faster than others. The best groups should be those that have worked as a team and sorted out their difficulties efficiently. They will have adapted their approach in the light of the new problems that faced them.

If the children are allowed to go round the room and look at each other's work, they should be able to spot some common features in the successful 'contraptions'. The triangles are an obvious one but can they distinguish the stronger part of the structure near the wall? (It may be that this is where the structure has begun to collapse.)

**SCIENCE PRINCIPLES TO HAVE IN MIND**
- Rigid triangular shapes and the problem of buckling will be met.
- Can the children spot that some of their struts are in tension and some in compression? Which of these is likely to fail first? How can this failure be prevented? Another way of putting this is to ask if any struts could be replaced by a piece of string with no loss of support.
- Engineers talk of *redundant members* of a structure — struts that are, in fact, doing nothing. Do your children have any of these? Can they be removed?

# UNIT 4
## Tower of strength

The next challenge is an old favourite with problem setters. It involves building a tower as tall as possible to hold a certain mass. This tower is to be built out of seemingly weak paper straws which are fixed together with pieces of pipe-cleaner. It is a suitable challenge for pairs of children working on a protected desk top.

The drinking straw gains its strength from its tubular shape, so this would be a good opportunity to discuss other structures made of tubes.

Why a tube? Well, it can resist bending in any direction. It resists the tendency to twist, and, of course, it is light because there is nothing in the middle! Where do we find tubes for strength? The stems of plants, bicycle frames, bones, baby-buggies, cane furniture, scaffolding, metal ladder rungs and felt-tip pens. Tubes can stand on their own, as in the line post, or be part of a complicated framework, as in a climbing frame.

*straws can be bent / cut* *three only for joints*

Towers need wide bases so that they do not topple over. The struts at the bottom carry the most weight so they are going to be the thickest. Also, when strong winds catch a tower, the greatest bending force will be at the base. Can the children spot these various features in photographs and slides of, for instance, the Eiffel tower or an electricity pylon?

You may prime the children with these ideas of strength and stability or you may decide to let them find these things out as they attempt to solve the next problem.

*Using only paper straws of any length you choose, build a tower as high as you can that will support a 100 g mass. The mass may be suspended from the top of the tower by a thread or sit on a platform at the top of the tower.*

The straws can be securely fixed together by a simple and effective method which you should now teach the children. Small lengths of pipe cleaner about 3 or 4 cm long should be used. Each straw that is joined at a corner must have two ends of a pipe cleaner stuck into it (figure 6). It may seem a little confusing at first but the children will soon pick it up. (Make sure *you* have had a bit of practice beforehand!)

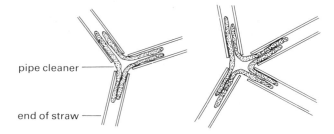

pipe cleaner

end of straw

**6** Fixing the straws with short lengths of pipe cleaner

This method of jointing ensures that the vertices can be easily taken apart and reassembled with an extra straw in place. Furthermore, when some of the struts in the tower are in tension (being stretched) the double pipe-cleaner fitting will generally hold tight.

The pipe cleaners are easily bought at a tobacconists and can be cut into pieces with a pair of scissors, or better still with a pair of pliers with wire cutters. If you have difficulty in finding pipe cleaners, then twisted pieces of paper straw will make a suitable but second rate substitute.

Loading the tower with the 100 g mass may cause

problems. If the children want a platform on top of their tower, then give them a piece of stiff card to place their mass on. If the tower comes to a point, then the mass will have to be hung from the top with a thread. The mass, however supported, should be lowered on to the tower gently as the children look for signs of weakness. If they see their tower failing at a particular point, then the loading can be stopped and remedial action taken before too much damage is done.

Can the children transfer the knowledge gained about triangular frameworks in the cantilever challenge? Perhaps they will have to learn the principle over again but it will certainly be useful in this exercise.

**7** How tall can you build a straw tower?

## Extension work

The children can always be encouraged to build their tower higher or perhaps to strengthen parts of it so that it can hold a greater mass. If a tower has completely collapsed and the children have become despondent, then challenge them to build a platform 10 cm high to hold as large a mass as possible.

## Summary

If you have made this challenge into a light-hearted competition, then the children will be interested to see who has done the best. Compare the lengths of the struts and the style of construction in the most successful towers with those that did not do so well.

---

**SCIENCE PRINCIPLES TO HAVE IN MIND**
- **Triangular shapes are rigid.**
- **Tubes have bending strength.**
- **Paper tubes are strongest in tension and weakest in compression.**
- **Towers need a stable base.**
- **Symmetry plays an important part in the overall strength of a tower.**

# UNIT 5
## Keep it up

The children, so far, have learnt how paper can be folded to support a mass, how card can be angled to give it more strength and how tubes can play an important part in forming strong frameworks. They will also have experienced the importance of rigid triangular shapes, especially when the joints of a structure are not rigid themselves. When they built their straw tower they probably found that the addition of a diagonal in a rectangular section of the frame prevented collapse. Remind the children of these principles now, because they should be able to apply all of them to the following challenge.

Make a structure that holds a marble out as far as possible from the edge of your desk. Your model must not in any way be fixed to the desk. You may use only four sheets of A4 paper, one sheet of card, 15 cm by 15 cm, and glue or sticky tape.

The distance from the desk can be measured horizontally outwards.

Once again the competitive element may inspire the children or you may choose to play this aspect down. If you have children who continuously find they are failing at these tasks, then be prepared to set them an easier brief. For instance, you might arrange for a less able group of children to begin with a large card box from which they build outwards. You will have overcome the problem of making a stable base and left them to think about an arm or cantilever to hold their marble away from the desk.

Most of your children, however, should have no difficulty in first of all constructing a base and then building out from it. Will they remember Challenge 1 when they built a tower with only one sheet of A4 paper? Will they remember the research they did for the egg box when they found that two strips of card at right angles to each other were particularly strong? Will they use tubes in their construction and will they remember their experiences with the cantilever when the part attached to the wall had to be the strongest?

Besides building something strong enough to hold the marble outwards, the children will have another problem to face that will be new to them. They will find, of course, that the marble tends to overbalance the structure. How will they counteract this? The card has been supplied for this purpose. If it is reasonably thick card, it will be about as heavy as the marble. Whether or not you suggest this to the children depends on their ability to work it out for themselves. If they begin to use the card in the main framework, they may find it difficult to remove it later when they need it. If you prefer to let them make this mistake at first, you could have a second piece of card ready to give to them when they ask for it. Alternatively, get them to suggest in the preliminary discussion ways of overcoming the problem of overbalancing and point out how important it is to think ahead.

**8** Putting their model to the test

## Extension work

If the children press hard for more of the same thing, ask them to fulfil the same brief using only paper straws and pipe-cleaners with the addition of one more marble for the counterbalance.

## Summary

In their work the children will have moved towards a better understanding of balance. If the base of the structure is broad, then it will probably be easier to keep upright. If the counterbalance is close to the base, it will not be as effective as it would be further away. These new ideas, as well as the ones previously met, should be discussed with the children as they inspect each other's models. Sometimes only an intuitive feel for a scientific principle will have been gained and, now, putting it into words will help the child accommodate the idea into his or her personal view of the world.

---

**SCIENCE PRINCIPLES TO HAVE IN MIND**
- **The point of balance is called the *fulcrum*.**
- **Balancing moments: force × distance is the same on both sides of the fulcrum for a static structure.**
- **The *centre of gravity* of a body is the point at which the whole weight of the body can be taken as acting.**
- **If the weight of the whole structure acts downwards outside the base, then the structure will topple over.**

## *UNIT 6*
### *Bridging the gap*

The final challenge in this topic is about bridge building. If you have not done so already, now is the time to show children pictures and slides of bridges or better still the real thing. A historical perspective would be particularly appropriate at this point. From clapper bridges to suspension bridges, the children will benefit from looking at a wide variety of structures that have been built through the ages. Their models may reflect this stimulating input if it is provided early on.

 *Using either (a) straws and pipe cleaners or (b) angled card strips with paper fasteners, build a bridge to span 70 cm from one desk to the next. Your bridge should not be fixed to the desks but simply rest on them. Your bridge should be strong enough to hold about 100 g at its centre.*

An example of the angled pieces of card that the children can use is shown in figure 9. You might expect children to make their own as they need them or, alternatively, you could prepare the struts yourself beforehand. It might help the children if you specify a maximum length for the struts.

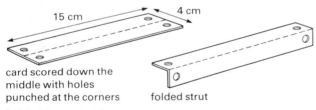

**9** Making a bridge strut

The holes punched in these strips enable them to be attached to other strips with paper fasteners in a number of ways (figure 10).

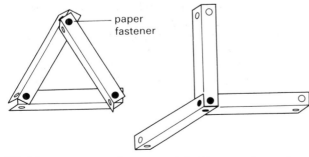

**10** The struts can be assembled in a variety of ways

### Bridge types

You may wish to talk to the children about the four main types of bridge: the beam, the arch, the cantilever and the suspension bridge. You may also want to go into detail about the kinds of building materials used and so on, but keep in mind that our main objective is to have the children learning to solve problems in a practical situation rather than learning facts about bridges.

The kind of structure that the children are about to build will almost certainly be a glorified beam bridge in the form of a truss. That is a rigid framework that is capable of sitting astride a gap without bending too much. They may incorporate the principle of the arch in their design but the base of an arch has to be anchored somehow or it will slide outwards and anchorage will be difficult in this brief as the bridge must rest freely on the desks. (The only way an arch could be supported here would be to construct a 'tie' joining the two bases of the arch and thus preventing them from sliding apart.) A cantilever structure would only be possible if large stable towers could be constructed at each end of the bridge and this is unlikely. In reality the children will be trying to construct a framework that acts somewhat like a plank of wood that might be thrown down to bridge a stream.

### Where will it break?

If we start to cross a ditch or stream by walking over a plank which then gives way, the break will almost certainly be at its centre. This will happen not as we step on to the plank but when we reach its centre. If the children think back to the research they did for the egg box, they will remember that the card struts they tested were loaded at the middle — the position at which most damage would be done.

What actually happens when a beam gives way at its centre? The children can find this out for themselves by taking an ordinary rubber or piece of rubber tubing and bending it as though it were a bridge holding a load. They will see that the top of the rubber is in compression and that the base is in tension. If they draw a small circle in ball point pen on the top of the rubber and another underneath, they will see the 'squeeze' and 'stretch' more clearly (figure 11).

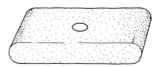 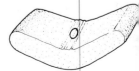

**11** Use a rubber to demonstrate bending forces

Take a small twig and snap it almost in half (figure 12). Where does the twig first begin to break? The children should find that this happens on the underside of the twig near the centre.

**12** The underside of a twig will snap first

When the children build their bridges they should keep these ideas in mind. They should perhaps expect to strengthen their bridge at its centre by using more struts or by making it wider, and they should remember that the bottom of their construction will be subject to tension forces while the top will tend to push together in compression.

## Team work

If you arrange your children in large groups of, perhaps, four or five, then they will need to organise themselves so that no-one is standing idle. There is much to be said for allowing them time to plan their design on paper and, just as important, to decide beforehand on the allocation of specific jobs to the various group members. For instance, the bridge will probably have two identical sides connected by cross struts and these can be made by two teams of children. Different members of the group could take it in turns to mass produce the card struts or the correct length straws. If you put a time limit on construction, then efficient group organisation and cooperation become all the more important.

Naturally, the construction of the bridge will take a fair amount of time. Be prepared to store the unfinished bridges at the end of the lesson if necessary. Alternatively, change the brief to suit the conditions and ask the children to construct the longest possible bridge that supports its own weight in the time allowed. This bridge could be built on the desk top with each end of the structure supported on a pile of books. The books can be moved outwards as the bridge grows. Of course, you would need to establish that the span of the bridge is the distance between the supports and not the length of the structure itself.

## Extension work

With a problem of this size, the children are more likely to need more time to complete the bridge rather than additional work. If they think they have finished, encourage them to make their bridge

stronger so it can hold a greater mass. How can this be done? Add more struts? Double up on some weak parts of the construction or replace weakened struts?

Could particularly able children continue the construction of their bridge until it spans 1 m?

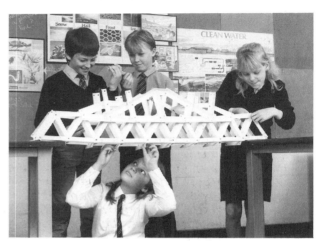

**13** Putting the finishing touches to a bridge built with card struts

## Summary

Perhaps each group could prepare a report on the construction of the bridge. What were the difficulties they met in deciding how to do it and in putting it together? If they could do it again, what would they change? If their bridge were gradually loaded with more and more masses, where do they think the bridge would fail first? Has the group followed any particular pattern in the construction of its model — are shapes in the bridge repeated — or is the structure a random one? If you have examples of both in the room then which are the more effective?

**SCIENCE PRINCIPLES TO HAVE IN MIND**
- **The critical point at which to load a beam with a single mass is at its centre.**
- **A loaded beam will have areas of tension and compression and these often have to be reinforced.**
- **The longer the span of a bridge, the stronger its construction needs to be.**
- **Angled struts or tubes combine strength with lightness — two features essential in bridge building.**

# Index